YOGA FOR PEACE

K.V. Raghupathi

ABHINAV PUBLICATIONS

abhinav publications

New Delhi

Cataloging in Publication Data—DK
Courtesy: D.K. Agencies (P) Ltd. <docinfo@dkagencies.com>

Raghupathi,K.V. (Kota Varadarajulu), 1957-.
Yoga for peace / K.V. Raghupathi
p. cm.
Articles; some previously published.
Includes index.
ISBN 817017483X

1. Yoga. I. Title.

DDC 181.45 22

First published in India 2007

Publishers
Shakti Malik
Abhinav Publications
E-37, Hauz Khas
New Delhi-110016 (INDIA)
Phones: 26566387, 26524658, 41655758
Fax: 91-11-26857009
e-mail: shakti@nde.vsnl.net.in
website: http://www.abhinavexports.com

ISBN 81-7017-483-X

Phototypesetting in Baskerville12 pt by
Laxmi Advertising
Sector-8, Rohini, Delhi

Printed at
D.K. Fine Art Press Pvt. Ltd.
Ashok Vihar, Delhi

CONTENTS

PREFACE

This volume has twenty essays, a few of them have been published in the *Vedanta Kesari* (Ramakrishna Math, Chennai) and *Saptagiri* (TTD Publication, Tirupati) over a period of six years. The essays *Spiritual Value of Yama, Spiritual Value of Niyama, Sthira Sukham Āsanam, Prānāyāma, Pancha Klēsas, Pancha Vrittīs, Nava Viksēpas, Two Kinds of Yogis, Two Kinds of Samādhi* and *Karma and Yoga* are the condensed forms of my talks on the first two parts (*Samādhi Pāda* and *Sādhana Pāda*) of Patanjali's *Yoga Sūtras* which I delivered at Sri Aurobindo Society, Tirupati in 2003-2004 with a view to correct and dispel certain distortions and misconceived ideas of yoga as it is practised and imparted by certain yogic schools which have come up like mushrooms in our country and encashed on it by offering different kinds of modified versions of yoga in different bottles. In these so-called schools and institutes yoga is viewed, understood and practised only from the health point. Unfortunately, this sacred holistic science has been reduced to a mere mockery of acrobatics. It has been reduced to a mere therapeutic drug sold in the market. What is more ridiculous is that competitions are held at district, state and national levels and prizes are given to the best performers of āsanas. Amidst this pulp and pseudoism the real prey is our own original yogic science as given by Patanjali two thousand years ago. It is with a view to retrieve this lost pure tradition I took up the venture of delivering talks to a limited enlightened audience when the invitation came to me from the trustees of Sri Aurobindo Society at Tirupati where I live. The offer provided me a wonderful opportunity to speak out the pure yoga which was given to the humanity by the great sage, Patanjali. The audience was very receptive and they received my talks with great enthusiasm and high spirit of understanding. Although I could not reproduce my original talks, word by word, which would have run into several hundreds of pages if I had done so, I honestly believe that the condensed form would unfailingly meet the requirement and serve the purpose. With this stout belief and constant hope, I have tried to convey the essence as it is found in the aphorisms without distorting it.

In the first essay *Yoga for an Integrated Life,* the importance of our ancient Yoga in achieving an integrated and harmonious life has been stressed. The second essay *Yoga and Western Psychology* traces the history and development of Western Psychology, brings out the shortcomings in it and points out how the ancient Yoga of our tradition has surpassed it by transcending the mind. The third essay *Dimensions of Yoga* deals with various false notions associated with it. In the fourth essay *Therapeutic Values of Yama and Niyama,* the ethical and medicinal value of Yama and Niyama in spiritual life has been presented in detail.

The significance of ten cardinal virtues of *Yama* and *Niyama* in the context of spiritual life has been brought out in the next two essays, *Spiritual Value of Yama* and *Spiritual Value of Niyama.* The third important limb āsana and what exactly it stands for as it is given in the original text *Yoga Sūtras* has been succinctly explained in the essay *Sthira Sukham Āsanam.* In *Prānāyāma* its importance in the practice of yoga as expounded by Patanjali, its functions, kinds and its benefits have been discussed elaborately.

Pancha Vrittīs examines the five modifications as given by Patanjali in his *Sūtras* and the methods of elimination. *Pancha Klēsas* deals with the five causes of misery and their removal. In the essay *Nava Viksēpas*, nine forms of disturbances that come in the way of meditation and the ways by which they can be overcome have been presented in greater detail. In *Two Kinds of Yogis*, the differences between Bhava Pratyāya Yogis and Upaya Pratyāya Yogis have been discussed. *Two Kinds of Samādhi* deals with Samprajnatha Samādhi and Asamprajnatha Samādhi as dealt with by Patanjali. The Doctrine of Karma, its implications, various kinds of Karmas and how Yoga can break the cycle have been dealt with elaborately in *Karma and Yoga.*

In *Yogic Walking for Relaxation* a new idea of yogic walking has been presented. Aspects like how it should be done and how total relaxation can be achieved have been explained. *Yoga and Ayurveda* deals with their importance from the point of health.

The idea that Ayurveda can be a companion Science to yoga and how Ayurveda can help sādhakas in their yogic life have been discussed. In *Yoga: A Science of Relaxation* a comprehensive approach to it has been presented. *Food and Yogic Sādhana* emphasises the importance of Satvic food in yogic sādhana. *Yoga as an Art of Social Reconstruction* deals with yoga from the artistic perspective. It is the greatest of all great arts because it essentially deals with human life in its totality. *Yoga and Peace* expounds how yoga can be used to achieve not only individual peace but also world peace.

TIRUPATI **K.V. RAGHUPATHI**

ACKNOWLEDGEMENTS

I owe thanks to the editors of *The Vedanta Kesari,* a publication of Sri Ramakrishna Math, Chennai and *Saptagiri* of Tirumala Tirupati Devasthanams for publishing a dozen essays and permitting me to publish them here. I am especially indebted to the trustees of Sri Aurobindo Society, Tirupati for providing me a wonderful opportunity and a platform to present the great secrets hidden in Patanjali's *Yoga Sūtras* in an objective way.

TIRUPATI **K.V. RAGHUPATHI**

1

YOGA FOR AN INTEGRATED LIFE

Today, man is at the crossroads. In spite of all the achievements he has made in the last few hundred years that added to the growth of civilization, he has to grow psychologically and spiritually. Morally and spiritually, he has become debased and decadent. He is highly divided and fragmented on petty things, and too narrowly compartmentalised in his outlook and understanding. He is pursuing his own maddening ends on different lines with justified or unjustified means at different levels without rendering an ear or an eye to what is happening around and to his own declining state. It is a sad commentary on man's life which, having caught in a world of consumerism, garish and antidiluvian and anachronistic values and ideas, has become deeply unconcerned, insensitive, apathetic, cruel and brutal in all respects of his living and thus has lost the fragrance of life in every sense. What is seen all around is not love but hatred, not peace but mutual bickerings and recriminations, not freedom but slavery to one's own ambitions, paranoic pursuits, not harmony but violence, not order but disintegration, not integrity in one's living but hypocrisy, not plainness but corruption.

The relevance of yoga is intensely felt in the context of prevailing hatred, disharmony and violence in the society, hopelessness that faces large blocks of humanity and the dire need of fresh ideas and new spring of optimism to motivate man and rouse the latent energies of all mankind. A great deal of violence in the society is due to division of humanity and man's identification with castes, communities, regions, sects, cults and various other groups. Fragmentation is rooted in our thinking and living which has generated more hatred, disharmony and misunderstanding than love and understanding. Too many ideals and goals, thoughts and ideas, institutions and associations, sects and groups have generated more animosity and hatred, and widened the hiatus between man and man. Man is simply reduced to a mere thing in his ideas and thoughts, goals and aspirations, dogmas and beliefs, traditions and conventions. On the other hand, man is a single indivisible being. So also existence, which encompasses every bit of creation. All differences and distinctions persist because of the way we look at, perceive and record our impressions. Otherwise, life is a single, unified force, Existence is whole. If this simple truth that underlies all life forces is at once perceived, recognised not without academically trained intellect but with deep insight and understanding, certainly we can create heaven not only in our life but for all on this most beautiful planet. Yoga achieves this synthesis, fruition and happiness.

Yoga has greater relevance than any other branch of science that has brought misery along with knowledge. If all knowledge goes in one direction, yoga synthesises and integrates. Yoga is a science of sciences. It is not a religion or a dogma or a creed, but a way of life. The foundation of all systems of knowledge is yoga. While the foundation of yoga is experience, Yoga is an experience, it is not knowledge. Though it is gained through experience, such knowledge cannot be imparted. At the core it is an experience, a great inexplicable experience. And this experience is non-transmittable and non-transferable. It is purely individual. But, through this individual experience, a yogi achieves universal experience.

What is yoga? The term 'Yoga' comes from the Sanskrit word '*yuj*' which means 'to join'. In its spiritual sense, it is the process by which the individual identifies with the cosmic. Ultimately, yoga means union with the infinite. The ultimate goal of yoga is to realize this cosmic unity within oneself and live in it constantly, every moment. Such a person may be called as an integrated, undivided whole being. He achieves harmony, unity, peace and happiness in his life. He radiates harmony, peace and happiness to his own surroundings. Thus, a yogi brings in a great peace for the whole humanity.

Harmony is yoga. Unity is yoga. Attaining integrity in one's life is yoga. It is rediscovering oneself. It is knowing one's own true nature, that is, *Sat-Chit-Ananda.* It is becoming one with the whole cosmic consciousness. It is unity, homogeneity, sameness with the Absolute. In Patanjali's *Yoga Sūtras* it is stated: "At the time of union, the seer (*Purusha*) rests in His own unmodified state." In *Dattatreya*

Samhita, it is defined as: "*Savachinta partiyagat nischinta yoga unchyute*—the state wherein there is no *Sankalpa-Vikalpa* as a result of renouncing the formative will, is termed Yoga." Again it is defined: "*Yoga Samādhih samatavastha Jivatma-Paramatmanoh*—*Jivatman* becomes identical with Brahman. That is Yoga." The *Bhagavad Gita* says: "*Yogat karmasu kausalam*—Yoga is skill in action", and "*Samatvam yoga uchyate*—equilibrium is called yoga".

Every human being has within himself tremendous potentialities and capacities for growth of which he is not aware. He is intelligent and divine. He is cosmic in miniature. He is infinite in finite. He is not merely a rational creature. More than this, he is spiritual, divine. He is the manifestation of that power and knowledge. As he evolves he unfolds new powers, new faculties, new qualities. By rediscovering himself, he can change his destiny. He can change and subdue his environment. He can influence nature and environment. He can be a master of internal and external nature. He can awaken these dormant powers through the practice of yoga. He can really become a highly evolved, synthesised, integrated human being, indeed a divine being. That is what Sri Aurobindo aimed at. Also other great mystics in this country.

Yoga is a science of sciences. It is a perfectly practical system of self-culture. One can attain a harmonious development of body, mind and soul. It is an exact science, a perfect science, a divine science. It is a science of experience in which *Jivatman* is merged with the *Paramatma.* It is not mere physical or breathing acrobatics or demonstrations of magic of supernatureal powers. It is the conquering of mind, subduing of mind. It is an experience of Mind within mind. It is, Patanjali says, *citta-vrittī-nirodhah*—thereby one attains *Sat-Chit-Ananda* (Knowledge-Existence-Bliss). He brings a message of hope to the forlorn, joy to the depressed, strength to the weak and knowledge to the ignorant. Yoga is the secret master key that unlocks the realm of Elysian bliss and deep abiding peace.

A yogi always keeps a balanced mind in all conditions of life and at all moments. He is a *Sthita Prajna.* His vision is deeply penetrating, he radiates joy, strength and vigour like the sun, attracts like a magnet. He will have great influence over the people with whom he comes into contact. One can attain physical and mental efficiency through yoga. An harmonious development of body, mind and soul can be attained through yoga. Happiness is man's nature. Peace is his quality. Harmony is his state. Strength is his heritage; efficiency not inefficiency; courage, not fear; bliss, not sorrow; knowledge, not ignorance; immortality, not mortality.

Mind, according to science, is a kind of radiant matter; and it exists. Yogic science shatters this idea and proves that there is nothing like mind in any shape and form. It is a myth. It has no existence apart from *Vrittīs* (modifications or thoughts). It is the thought that plays the mischief. According to yogic philosophy mind minus *Vrittīs* is pure consciousness, all pervasive, devoid of form, eternal, radiant and transparent, mobile and immobile. According to science, nothing is free, everything is bound up in necessity. Necessary effects follow necessary causes. Scientists hold that the human mind cannot go beyond these unifying laws. The noumenon, the life-giving principle of laws, is a point where the scientific understanding stops. Anything beyond there is *terra incognita*. Yogic science goes beyond this false conclusion. It says it is the thinking ego tied down by the laws of necessity. Yoga tries to investigate this reflecting ego—the subject and the object seen are one and the same. It is this realization that releases man from the shackles of bondage. Further, it tries to investigate the principle of unity, which is the point of reference of all different existences and which transcends the apparent divinity of things. Owing to *Vrittī bheda*, mind acquires various forms. Otherwise it is pure consciousness (*chit*), *sattvic* and all-pervading.

Unlike other systems of Hindu philosophy, yoga is wholly practical. It is a natural science based on certain immutable Laws of Nature. It is the Science of sciences that disentangles the individual soul from the phenomenal world of sense-objects and links with the Absolute, whose inherent attributes are Infinite Bliss, Supreme Peace, Infinite Knowledge and Infinite Joy. Aiming at harmony is the goal of human life and that ought to become the touchstone of all human endeavours. That ought to be the be-all and end-all of existence. Yoga does not invent "the other" harmony or peace, or happiness or freedom. But, it helps one rediscover oneself—harmony which is substratum of all existence. Equanimity is yoga.

Serenity is yoga. Awareness is yoga. Anything by which the best and the highest in life can be attained is yoga. Yoga is thus all-embracing, all-inclusive and universal in its application leading to all-round development of human personality. It harnesses our will and emotions and expands our power of analysis, insights and visions. Such a science which harnesses the will, calms the mind and steadies the emotions is the key to human progress. Yoga is the right science for such a transformation which is in the offing. It is a science of the future with a holistic vision relevant to a progressive society.

Yoga is rooted in virtue. Ethical discipline is very essential for success in yoga. The value and importance of such ethical requirements is not to be neglected or underestimated, for, these moral qualifications, when in full bloom or developed to perfection, can even manifest as spiritual powers of a very high order, nay, they constitute a gateway to the immortal self. The two moral backbones of yoga are *Yama* and *Niyama*. These correspond to the Eightfold Path of Lord Buddha. They are: *satyam* (truthfulness), *āsteyam* (abstention from any tendency to steal), *ahimsā* (non-violence), *brahmacharyam* (celibacy) and *aparigraha* (abstention from coveting others' wealth and possession) are the five *Yamas*. *Saucham* (cleanliness and purity of mind and body), *santosa* (contentment), *tapas* (self-discipline), *svādhyāya* (engagement in study to keep self-realization) and *Ishvarapranidhana* (surrender to God's Will) are *Niyamas*. These *Yamas* and *Niyamas* eradicate all the impurities of the mind. In fact, *Yama* and *Niyama* form the corner-stones of yoga philosophy.

Yogāsanas restore the balance of the impaired homeostasis and tranquil the mind. Through *Prānāyāma* the imbalances at the subtler layers of our personality are set right paving the way to easy access towards the hidden potentialities of inner silence. The fifth limb *Pratyahara* increases the will power at the level of senses. In fact, all the five limbs—*Yama, Niyama, Āsanas, Prānāyāma* and *Pratyahara* enhance the "will power" inbuilt at our physical and physiological levels. The last three limbs *Dhārana, Dhyāna* and *Samādhi* enhance the will power at mental level. Thus, the eight-limbed *Astānga Yoga* caters to the entire Body-Mind complex and hence, is called the king among the yogas—*Raja Yoga.*

To conclude, in this age of perversity yoga has great relevance and applicability and it gives us an invigorating energy for harmonious, integrated and peaceful living. We have wide range of human knowledge and resources. We have gathered enough experience through science. We have adequate technology that can annihilate humanity. What we need is inner strength and development. We have miserably failed to evolve ourselves morally and spiritually. We have reached the state of neurosis and mood of paralysis. It is high time that we rediscovered ourselves, our inner strength and energy, our true nature being happiness and peace and become as wholesome creatures in the world. What is urgently needed to prove that we are basically humane, peaceful loving creatures, is a deep radical transformation in the context of human consciousness which alone can redeem ourselves from all evils that are purely inventions, plaguing and destroying. All other things, laws, propaganda, preachings, lectures and writings will not help us and save us. These may touch the periphery of human mind, but not the heart. It is the metamorphosis in human psyche that changes one's life and human destiny. All other changes and reformations are purely social and political external to man and transient in nature. It is the internal change that must take the course of human life. This metamorphosis can be brought through the practice of yoga. Yoga brings a deep abiding change in human consciousness. Yoga helps us see what we are, who we are, where we are, how we are, and transcends us beyond all illusions, hallucinations and delusions, and makes us true human beings on the earth. Yoga shows us the path out of confusion. It makes us fully integrated, wholesome beings.

Is life worth living? Yes, indeed. Life is worth living. Life is beautiful. Life is meant for living, peacefully and happily. No sorrow is embedded in life. It is wonderful and lovely. Yoga gives such boundless optimism, hope and faith in living. A true yogi enjoys himself, basking in the light and glory of life. He obeys the laws of his being as well as the universe, enjoys self-content, gladness of soul and enthusiasm which cannot be explained by the mere possessions of physical wealth. These highest and purest attainments of the human soul are not the results of mere physical well-being, but of the peace and harmony which come only through obedience to natural laws. A true yogi enjoys such peace as long as he breathes. Such is the *peace which passeth understanding.*

2

YOGA AND WESTERN PSYCHOLOGY

Psychology is the proper study of mind, more particularly human behaviour. Man is an evolving creature. In the process of evolution over a million years, man's psyche has undergone a radical change, from the state of dormancy to a state of activity. With the evolutionary change of mind, man has brought in myriad creations. Today, the map of physical world has been totally changed; a change that had never been witnessed or dreamed of in the past. All this change, it is true, has brought more comforts and luxuries to himself. At the same time, man has become a complex creature. His mind has become so complex and perplexing that he began examining and studying his own mind, its nature and complexities. Thus, the science of psychology has come to stay.

When we refer to psychology, we obviously mean psychology that is taught and studied in academic institutions rather than individual oriented. Also, we identify psychology that has come from the West, known as Western psychology. Indeed, this science was born in the West and later developed and nurtured before it had been spread to the Eastern world. All theories and concepts and schools have been developed in the West. Today, in all academic institutions, these theories and concepts are taught with much enthusiasm and devotion.

Western Psychology until Freud came to the scene was treated as a part of philosophy. In other words, it became an exclusive privilege of philosophers to study psychology. These two sailed together in the academic world. But, after Freud, everything was changed. Psychology was separated from philosophy and it became a new subject of interest. Nevertheless, its umbilical links could not have been snapped from philosophy. Sufficient to say, psychology is deeply embedded in philosophy. And Western psychology has its roots in Western philosophy.

Nineteenth Century saw the foundations of the experimental psychology, a landmark in the history of Western psychology. Until then psychology was purely subjective. Later, psychology was influenced by new discoveries in physics, chemistry and biology. A number of psychological doctrines were based on the theory of evolution as prescribed by Lamarck, Darwin, Galton and Spencer. The method of introspection gave way to the method of experimentation.

The Twentieth Century saw the development of diverse systems of psychology. Watson's Behaviourism tries to explain mental phenomenon through stimulus and response. According to him mental activities are performed mechanically and there is nothing like consciousness. He said that human character is known by behaviour alone. Then came McDougall's 'Purposive Psychology' or 'Hormic Psychology', which distinguishes human activity and mechanical activity, the former is characterised by 'free-will'. According to him, life is teleological. He strongly refuted Materialistic mechanism. The 'Analytic Psychology' which emphasises each type of mental activity has been corrected by the 'Gestalt Psychology' which laid emphasis on the synthetic whole, as opposed to the parts. It is the total personality that thinks, feels and acts. But, all these schools lack the proper explanation of the totality of human mind, and its various states like conscious, unconscious and superconscious.

Interestingly, all these schools were chiefly concerned with the conscious mind only. They have failed to explain the mental behaviour stored in the unconscious. We owe a lot to Sigmund Freud (1856-1940) for his discovery of the unconscious, and later to Alfred Adler (1870-1937) and C.G. Jung for further exploration in this direction and for enlivening and enriching the school of Psycho-analysis. Freud's discoveries constitute a landmark in the history of Western Psychology. But both Freud and Adler have missed the fundamental source of unconscious behaviour. They exaggerated the instincts of sex and self-assertion respectively. Jung traces the behaviour to the racial past and opens fresh vistas for Racial Psychology.

The chief methods employed by Western psychologists to prove human behaviour are:

Introspection, Observation, Experimental and Analytical. The methods of observation and experimentation have been substituted by Psycho-analysis and Introspection. With all this proliferation of different schools of psychology and the availability of a vast body of literature, psychology in the West has failed to understand and explain the fundamental source of all human behaviour.

Western Psychology is a product of Western Philosophy. It is based on the Western materialistic philosophy. It suffers from certain limitations. The most prominent are: *First*, it has unfortunately abandoned the method of Introspection which is a fundamental source for understanding human psyche in its proper manner. *Second*, Western psychology has studied the wakeful state of conscious level of mind. It has never studied the original source, the Super-conscious state which is outside its purview. *Third*, Western psychology does not study man as a whole. On the contrary, it studies mind as a single separate phenomenon. *Fourth*, the Western psychology does not accept the infallibility of reason beyond a certain point. It fails to go beyond the perception of senses. Further, the West is under the false notion that no man can ever transcend the bonds of physical perceptions. *Fifth*, the Western psychology studies stream of consciousness, a concept developed by William James and later promoted by Jung. One or two questions may be asked here: What causes the continuity of experience? How does a person know that the experiences of today and yesterday belong to the same person? The concept of stream cannot explain this phenomenon. *Sixth*, the problem of nature and origin of mind has never been explained by the psychologists in the West to satisfaction of the Eastern mind. Behaviourists like Watson, Pavlov, Max Mayer, Franz and others talked of behaviour only. Psychologists like Freud, Adler and Jung were not unanimous about the source of human mental behaviour. Materialist biologists assert the various stages of material complexity. It is a well known fact in the East that human mind works at a deeper level than at the perceptual level of stimulus and response. *Seventh,* all scientific discoveries in the West conclude that there is nothing like mind apart from the nervous system and brain. Such a conclusion is far from truth. If this conclusion is accepted, then, the world would be altogether different. No Buddha or Christ or no mystic would have been needed to relieve humanity from suffering. Further, the scope of treatment of psychological disorders through physiological operations like electro-therapy is extremely limited. As such the nervous system cannot explain the root causes of the psychological disorders and mental diseases. *Eighth,* all the Western psychologists have failed to give any satisfactory explanation of the mind-body relationship. The dialectic materialists' philosophy which says that man is not a complex machine, the Epiphenomenalism which says that mental events are the byproducts of bodily events, and the Interactionism explained by Descrates (1596-1650) which says that body is the extended substance of mind have failed to give a cogent explanation of the relationship between body and mind. *Ninth,* all phenomena of Extra-Sensory-Perception (ESP) such as telepathy, clairvoyance, clairaudience, precognition, mesmerism, dream-visions, apparitions, ghosts, psychometry, psychokinesis, telekinesis, levitation, etc., have not been recognized in normal psychology of the West. They constitute a separate branch of study called 'Para Psychology'. For a long time this science has not been recognized and treated as a subject. *Tenth,* the dream phenomenon is still a puzzle to the Western psychologists. Though Freud, Adler and Jung have discovered the subconscious thoughts playing their part in the dreams, they have failed to give proper explanation for the prophetic dreams and many other such dreams. Some complex questions may arise here: What are the physiological organs that function while dreaming? Are the dream perceptions real or illusory? What is the relation between deep sleep state and dream state? What is the relationship between the wakeful state and dream state? Who dreams? Who experiences dream perceptions? How does ESP function in dreams? How are dreams connected with the individual's past birth and future life? These and many other such questions have remained as riddles to the Western psychologists even today.

What the Western psychology has failed to explain the nature of mind in its proper perspective, Indian psychology provides us clearcut answers to many baffling questions. Indian psychology is embedded in Indian philosophy. No aspect of human life and the universe has been left unexamined by Indian saints, sages and philosophers. While Western psychology is an offshoot of Western philosophy and science, Indian psychology emerges from Indian philosophy. It surpasses Western psychology in scope, methodology and validity of conclusions. It solves a number of problems concerning psychology, which remain unsolved in the West.

Philosophy in India has been treated as '*Darsana*' which means 'vision', 'insight', intuition' and thus the word itself signifies that Indian philosophers pursued the quest of having a total vision of life and universe, based on personal experience. With the faculty of intuition (which is over and above reason), the Indian philosophers looked at the cosmos as a whole and arrived at truth—that there exists supreme consciousness which is the source of all that constitutes the Universe, designated as 'Brahman' or Ultimate Reality in the *Upanishads*; it is the essence of living and there exists a direct relation between the individual and this consciousness. This consciousness pervades the entire Universe, and it animates both organic and inorganic matter. The difference in degree of life is mainly due to the degrees in the quantum of consciousness and its threefold nature or *guna* (*sātvika, rājasika* or *tāmasika*). The *Upanishads* proclaim that all life is product of Consciousness (*Purusha*) and matter. Matter is insentient without *Purusha.* The subject of Indian psychology is, therefore, consciousness proper, that is the be-all and end-all of all life and thought. Another epistemological truth is the nature of knowledge and its valid sources. Indian philosophy classifies knowledge into three types: direct cognition (*pratyaksa*), inference (*parōksa*) and intuitive (*aparōksa*). It has demonstrated that individual mind can transcend the realms of limited cognition, and enter super-cognition or intuitional state.

Except Carvaka system (which is virtually non-existent) and Mimamsa, all the schools of Indian philosophy (Vedanta, Yoga, including Buddhism and Jaina) admit intuition. It does not mean intellect (*anumana, upamana, tarka*) is denied. But intuition presents truth of first order, and reason and experience present truth of the second order. There is no antithesis between the two. Reason is to be supplemented by intuition. Advaita talks of *Paramārthika satta* (intuition and superconsciousness) as the highest reality and it makes *Vyāvahārika satta* (empirical reality) subservient to intuition. Mind is something higher than nervous system. Objective method can work at the superficial level. Intuitional method will dive deep into the waters. All philosophical systems in India arose out of insight (*darsana*) and intuitive knowledge is beyond all proof (*pramanyam nirapeksam*).

Indian psychology is embedded in Indian philosophy. It is the science of consciousness and its scope is the study of consciousness which pervades the entire Universe. Indian psychology gives full account of not only the subconscious but of four gradual states, viz., Unconscious, Dream conscious, Conscious and Superconscious. Western psychology cannot approach the depths of mind through the objective methods employed in physical sciences. Experiments at the perceptual level may succeed, but for understanding the functioning of the higher faculties of mind like reasoning, judgements, imagination, talent, sentiment, will, devotion, tranquillity and equipoise, introspection suits. Observation and experimentation are confined to lower types of conscious behaviour. The introspection will examine all the four stages, viz., Unconscious, Conscious, Dream state and Superconscious. Every man can introspectively examine his own mind, analyse his mental tendencies, understand his weaknesses, control them, develop higher power and integrate the whole personality. This is the subject matter of Yoga.

The ontological, epistemological and psychological doctrines of Yoga are based on Samkhya system of philosophy. But, it deals with a number of subjects not dealt with in Samkhya. It begins where Samkhya ends. Samkhya emphasises knowledge as the means of release. The realization of Purusha that it is different from Prakriti, releases him from its bondage. But Yoga emphasises meditation as the means. The highest form of matter is *Citta,* and Yoga annihilates it by *Sādhana.*

Yogic psychology teaches detachment and dispassionate working of mind. Its object is to divest the mind of all its impurities. It destroys all the five *klesas,* namely, ignorance (*avidya*), egoism (*asmita*), attachment (*rāga*), aversion (*dvēsa*) and clinging to life (*adhinivesa*). Man is tossed between the two extremes of life, pleasure and pain, attraction and aversion, likes and dislikes. No psychologist tells us how to harmonise the two. Yoga tells us how to strike a balance in human life. The psychotherapy developed in the West has never solved human psychic problems. Yoga on the other has provided us remedy for all psychic and physical ailments. Yoga is far superior to psychoanalysis. In psychoanalysis the person approaches the analyst as a patient. He himself chalks out the programme of self-analysis and proceeds with yogic exercises for clearing and cleansing of the mento-emotional nature. Yoga has a goal, that is, liberation (*kaivalya*). Psychoanalysis has no goal, the patient is frustrated. Yoga does not emphasise religious practices, but devotion as a means of psychic progress. It is in a way an Analytical psychology. Both Yoga and Analytical psychology emphasise self-knowledge and self-analysis. Modern psychology deals with the superficial causes of any psychic ailment. But yoga suggests the destruction of deep-rooted tendencies and not merely suppression or redirection. The ultimate aim of yoga is to bring about complete transmutation of the substance of our nature. Yoga does not recommend temporary measures like removing temporary incidental causes. It aims at the destruction or total eradication of all mental modifications through will and practice, aided by yogic methods.

Yogic psychology is therefore higher psychology dealing with supermental states, or we may call it para psychology. It starts where the known psychology ends. It deals with all the states of consciousness-subconsciousness, consciousness and superconsciousness. It is both a positive science and normative science guiding the development of mental and spiritual potentialities.

3
DIMENSIONS OF YOGA

Yoga, one of the six orthodox systems of Indian philosophy developed by Patanjali in his *Yoga Sūtras,* aims at freeing the mind from pain arising from sins and sickness, from relations with living and non-living things. This is accomplished by non-attachment, purifying mind and body and discriminatory knowledge. The true purpose is to eliminate the *Vrittīs* (the modifications) of the mind and integrate man with the ever-present universal consciousness. This system which is considered as most complex, yet dynamic, has influenced not only the various forms of Hindu religious literature such as the *Purānas,* the *Tantras,* the *Mahābhārata,* the *Gītā,* the *Panchatantra* and other literature related to them, but also many of the Buddhist Tantras. The idea of the union of *Prakriti* and *Purusha* has also influenced various forms of worship, art and iconography. The medical science too has come under its influence.

Buddhism was introduced in Tibet about the seventh or eighth century. It came to be known as

Tibetan Buddhism, and was modified by various forms of local beliefs and faiths. There is a close affinity between the two forms, the Yoga system and the Tibetan Buddhism. The various typical geometrical forms representing the field of force of the different forms of the newly introduced divinities, known as *chakras* are otherwise identified with the six principal nerve plexuses described in *Yoga Sūtras* on which a yogi could concentrate and ultimately attain liberation.

Though the system has lost much of its pristine power, it has been preserved through the ages. Different religions may come and go but yoga exists for ever. But the sad part of it was that it became an exclusive privilege of the few. This science of sciences, the philosophy of philosophies, the religion of religions was shrouded in mystery and obscurity. Not many had the privilege to have access to it. As a result, today we hardly come across a single institution or a school or an individual who can provide us the knowledge of this great system in its totality. It has been reduced to a mere study of academic interest. Institutes have made it a subject of therapeutic value at physical level. It is sold like a commodity in different forms in cities by self-styled Yogis. People in sheer fascination learn it by paying a high price only to abandon at a later stage. Most of them are insincere and irregular in practising. They continue to live in their old habits. Today Yoga is regarded as a superior form of physical exercise.

Yoga is a holistic science. Mere *āsanas* are not Yoga. Acquiring knowledge about Yoga from books is not Yoga. By reciting some Sūtras without living a life also is not yoga. Yoga does not tell us what to do and what not to do, but 'how to be'.

It is true 'how to be' cannot be taught so easily in schools and colleges. Yoga teachers themselves do not practise it sincerely. They live contrary to the spirit of Yoga. What is taught in institutions is the knowledge of the outer world, and not the inner world. We hardly realize that there is one kind of education which is essential for the uplift of our personality, that is, inner education, to which we are never directed. It is never stressed. This inner education is the fundamental basis for man to lead a happy and peaceful life. This is not to say that the objective knowledge is superfluous. Yoga asserts that all knowledge proceeds from the subject, who is the knower. Yoga analyses and studies who this knower is. It makes us see the truth that the objective knowledge is transitory in nature, and hence, any adherence to it will only bring misery. For harmonious living both objective and subjective education are essential.

This inner education is 'self-education' which Yoga emphasises. What is this 'self-education'? It is not to learn from books and institutions, but being just what we are without altering our condition. This is 'to become aware of'. Yoga means 'self-awareness', awareness of ourselves. The purpose of Yoga is not to introduce ourselves to a vague concept of God but first and foremost to our own self. It is here that the real journey begins and it is endless.

This awareness is what is known as meditation.

Meditation does not mean sitting in a posture and concentrating on something or dwelling deep for a few minutes and later leading a contrary life the whole day. Yoga is meditation in action. It teaches how to conduct ourselves in this most complex world, how to respond to a situation, how to live in it, how to make the best out of it. A true yogi never creates a situation. On the contrary, he/she waits for it to arise. It is an eternal waiting and watching like a kingfisher perching on a branch near the pond. As the situation arises like a fish from the pond, the yogi plunges into it like the bird. It is this watching, being ever vigilant, during the interval between two situations that makes a yogi happy and well-composed. When the situation arises he faces it, lives in it completely without being tainted by it.

Yoga teaches us how to be independent. Being independent is doing everything for ourselves without relying on others. Nature has provided everything for sustenance of every creature. But man depends not only on others for sustenance but also on God for material benefits. Yoga doesn't teach us this.

True Yoga starts with *Yama* and *Niyama,* which are essential for attaining happiness and peace. In fact, following this discipline is of paramount importance in Yoga. It leads to spiritual discipline. What is first required is that yoga institutes must put the learners on spiritual discipline for some time before other limbs of *Astānga Yoga* are imparted. We have to see the need of urgency in transforming our life to make our life and the society better. First and foremost, our learning and living must start from here. If this is not done with seriousness, our life becomes meaningless.

Yoga teaches us how to live in the 'now' and not in the past or future. Both past and future are unreal, only 'now' is real. Even this also gradually vanishes. A true yogi lives in timelessness. He/she lives in this world and moves and interacts with people, practically he/she is never bound by such transitory elements.

Yoga teaches us how to respect life—the principle of life in other creatures. Though the forms are different, the life-force is the same. The moment this is realized, compassion flows copiously. The realized will respect every creature, adore it, or worship, and treat it as equal. He/she never does any harm by thought, word or action. As a result, all will coexist and live on the principle of mutual respect and love. This will bring in great happiness on the earth. Perfect ecological balance can be maintained.

This realization can come to anyone irrespective of age. All need to be transformed. There is no restriction that only the young should be transformed and not the old. But, it is much better if this transformation takes place at the very early age.

The young too must realize the immense values of life. Youth is the right time to cultivate all virtues. Young men and women should realize that life has a greater purpose imposed on them. It is only by living in virtue that one comes to understand what life is. Yoga helps one correct this behaviour. It helps achieve a perfect understanding of the body and mind. It plays a positive role in the development of an individual into an integrated personality.

4
THERAPEUTIC VALUES OF YAMA AND NIYAMA

Human life in modern society is complex. In the olden days life was said to be relatively peaceful, free from tensions, anxieties and depressions from which the present generation is suffering. Modern life has brought for world several types of challenges to man —climatic, infectional, physical and emotional. Emotional challenges relatively produce a much more powerful strain on the human system, in spite of the compensatory automatic processes in the body itself.

Harrison in the book *Principles of Internal Medicine* has identified the following as psychosomatic diseases: Peptic Ulcer, Mucous Colitis, Ulcerative Colitis, Bronchial Asthma, Atopic Dermatitis, Urtiricaria, Angino-Neurotic Oedema, Hay Fever, Raymond's Disease, Hypertension, Hyper Thyroidism, Amenorrhea and other diseases of Menstruation, Enwrisis, Dysuria, Paraxymal Tachycardia, Rheumatoid Arthritis and Migraine. Phychic stress produces Sinus, Tachycardia, Arthythurias, Coronary Spasm, Angina, Heart Attack and even sudden death.

Western scholars report that it has been clinically proved that states of mind like lust, anger, stress or depression affect the body's immune system and the robustness of the cardio-vascular system. These unkind states tend to increase blockage in the arteries, leading to heart diseases.

Causes of Ill-health

Statistical surveys by medical men show that 85 per cent of the cases of migraine, headache, 50 per cent of the cases of stomach ulcer, 75 per cent of the cases of gases in the intestines, and about 50 per cent of the cases of female diseases are emotionally induced. Appendicitis, usually regarded as a surgical case, may also be emotionally induced. Diabetes, unless due to a hereditary defect in the pancreas, is also emotionally caused. All asthma patients are emotionally disturbed. Anxiety and brooding nature are at the root of many incurable and chronic dispositions.

Brain surgery shows that even our old anxieties and emotions recorded in the thalamus and the hypothalamus are closely linked with our Autonomous Nervous System (ANS). It is this ANS that controls our internal vital formation like heart beating, breathing, intestinal action, endocrine glands, etc. These vital functions regarded as autonomous are usually affected by our negative thoughts, emotions and anxieties. Good emotions and thoughts produce a balanced and harmonious secretion from the glands. Bad emotions and thoughts produce more stress in the system. In fact, the Harvard medical school found that the single emotion most common, prior to a heart attack, was anger. A bout of anger lowers the pumping efficiency of the heart, resulting in drop in the blood flow to heart. These conclusions were also confirmed by independent studies conducted by Stanford and Yale medical schools. Medical evidence shows that next to anger comes depression as a contributor to such health problems. Stress significantly affects health and experiments showed that such emotions tend to double the risk of not only diseases but also asthma, ulcer, arthritis and headache. Under this stress, a malfunctioning of vital organs like lungs, heart and intestines may take place. Some of the negative emotions may have been recorded even in infancy. Such strong emotions may have been deeply planted in the subconscious state, which the psychologists call 'complexes'. The deeper and the more concealed an emotion, the more powerful and permanent the impact it might make on the whole system, which in turn may produce chronic, even life-long diseases. All stress ultimately acts like a challenge to human system.

Effect of Medicines

Tranquillizers are no real solution to these psychosomatic diseases. Their effect is transitory, deceptive and destructive. Some of these tranquillizers may cause jaundice, may have toxic effects. They interfere with the regular functioning of vital organs like heart, lungs and intestines. Other therapies in modern allopathic system are too individualistic, and do not take the whole system—body-mind mechanism

—into account. Further, medical drugs have a very long history of only suppressing the diseases or minimizing the effects, but not tackling the cause. The patient may not be aware of the real cause of the disease—the cause may be invariably some unhygienic food habits cultivated over a long period of time or unhealthy emotions.

The only correct remedy for these psychosomatic diseases is the replacement of wrong emotions by right emotions. In other words, we have to forsake all our negative emotions by cultivating positive emotions and thinking. By this, over 90 per cent of patients in modern society would probably get well without going to doctors for treatment. We can lead a relatively good and peaceful life. We have a system given by nature, which can work on its own without the interference of doctors and drugs. Maslow says organisms have their own biological wisdom. Such a system is inherent in all of us. But, unfortunately, as time passes, due to various cultural influences and customs imposed on us and due to personal habits, this fine natural system is totally disrupted leading to so many complexities.

Man is a single, undivided, unified distinct being in which no part of organism can be separated and studied in isolation. Body is as much important as mind. Mind can create a deeper impact on body than vice versa. Mind is very subtle, it is a bundle of thoughts, emotions and feelings. The whole yoga philosophy centres around this suitable part in human organism. It deals with how we can master this turbulent mind, subdue it in order to rise to greater spiritual heights and achieve cosmic union. All diseases originate from mind. The emotional disturbances finally manifest in the form of diseases in body. Unfortunately, all systems of modern treatment unduly focus attention on body but not on mind.

Yoga

Yoga is the inner core of Hindu religion. But it is not a religion by itself. It is the inward search for divinity, the sublime, and the bliss, the beyond, the infinite self, the substratum of the cosmos. It is meant for life here, and hereafter. It is vital for man, for his mental and physical health, his happiness, his efficiency, his creativity, and the self-actualization of his hidden genius. It is not to be attained but has to be regained. All of us have it, but owing to the defects of our upbringing, we have lost it. Yoga retrieves it.

In the *Astānga yoga* given by Patanjali, the first two limbs constituting *yama* (restraint) and *niyama* (self-discipline) are most important without which the practice of *āsana* (posture), *prānāyāma* (control of the life-force) *pratyāhāra* (self-withdrawal), *dhārana* (concentration), *dhyāna* (absorption) and *Samādhi* (ecstasy) will not yield any positive result. In fact, to do *dhyāna* a strict observance of *yama* and *niyama* is absolutely imperative. One who follows *yama* and *niyama* in practical life true to word and spirit will easily get installed in *dhyāna.* As his/her mind and body are purified, *dhyāna* naturally happens to him/her.

Role of Yama and Niyama

Under *yama* are subsumed five ethical rules which can be considered the fundamental property of all major religions. These are: *ahimsā* (non-hurting/non-killing), *satya* (truthfulness), *āsteya* (non-stealing), *brahmacharya* (brahmanic conduct i.e. chastity), *aparigraha* (greedlessness). These constitute the 'great vow' (*mahāvrata*) and in the *Yoga Sūtras* are enjoined to be practised irrespective of place, time, circumstances and one's particular social status. They are meant to bring under control man's life-style, which is seen as the root cause of his confusion, distress and suffering. Moral integrity is an indispensable prerequisite of successful yogic practice. Some yoga texts mention additional five ethical rules: *dayā* (compassion), *arjava* (uprightness), *kshama* (patience), *dhriti* (steadfastness) and *mitāhara* (temperance).

The most fundamental of all *yamas* is *ahimsā* or 'non-killing'. It is in fact non-violence in thought and deed. It is the root of all other ethical norms. *Satya* or 'truthfulness' is always exalted in the ethical and yogic literature. The *Mahānirvāna Tantra* (IV.75-6) emphasizes: 'no virtue is more excellent than truthfulness, no sin greater than (telling) untruth'. Therefore, the (virtuous) man should seek refuge in truthfulness with all his heart. Without truthfulness the recitation (of sacred *mantras*) is useless, without truthfulness austerities are as unfruitful as seed (which falls on) barren land. *Āsteya* or non-stealing is closely related to non-harming. It stipulates that any unauthorized appropriation of things of value from another causes that person pain. *Brahmacharya* or 'chastity' is of vital importance in yoga. *Aparigraha* or 'greedlessness' may be defined as the non-acceptance of gifts because this would create unnecessary attachment and fascination.

The five principles of *Yama* purify the mind from desire, anger and greed, whereas the five rules of *Niyama* or 'self-discipline' are intended to regulate our relationship with the transcendent reality. The five norms are: *saucha* (purity), *santōsa* (contentment), *tapas* (contemplation), *svādhyāya* (self-study), and *īshvara-pranidhāna* (devotion to the lord). *Saucha* or 'purity' is cleanliness in the widest possible sense, as bodily and mental purity. *Santōsa* or 'contentment' results from detachment from worldly objects. The person does not care for accumulation or securing of possessions, nor expects anything from anybody. He rests content with whatever comes his way. He does not crave for anything that is unnecessary. Even if he acquires wealth by right means, the surplus he may use for *loka kalyāna. Tapas* disciplines the body and emotions. However *tapas* should not deteriorate into senseless self-torture. Patanjali states quite plainly that properly executed, *tapas* strengthens and perfects the body (*Yoga-Sūtras* III.45-6). *Svādhyāya* or 'self-study' has a double aspect. It stands for the absorption into the sacred literature and for the simultaneous mental concentration and introversion and courageously face all aspects of one's nature in an honest attempt to 'know oneself'. *Īshvara-pranidhāna* or 'devotion to the lord' is defined in the *Yoga-Bhāshya* (II.32) as the 'offering of all deeds to the supreme teacher', which is the idea of *karmayoga* as expressed in the *Bhagvad-Gita*. The supreme teacher is of course the 'lord' (*īshvara*), the Transcendental Self. Elsewhere in the *Yoga-Bhāshya* (I.23) the *pranidhāna* is explained as 'special love' through which one gains the sympathy of the divine teacher who can speed up one's progress towards emancipation.

All the great religions have developed codes of conduct which help people to discipline themselves so as to create a semblance of order not only in the society but also within themselves. But the *Yamas* and *Niyamas* are unique for their grounding in cosmic spiritual laws. These are like 'dos' and 'don'ts'. They have tremendous therapeutic values. It may be said that yoga is self-administered, drugless psychotherapy. If adhered strictly in life, we can free ourselves from all the psychosomatic diseases and create a life of beauty, love, peace and freedom for ourselves which in turn will affect the whole society. Thus a paradise can be created here and now in this world. Disease is the violation of these laws, which are quite inherent in life. Man knows what he is doing. But he realizes this and recognizes the importance of *Yamas* and *Niyamas* late in his life. That is the real tragedy. By then he would have perished, left with little time and energy to pursue these laws. If this realization comes early in his life, it is better. He shall lead a harmonious life and make the best out of it.

Some people think that yoga begins with *dhyāna* or with *āsanas* or *Prānāyāma*. But these are the ones who live in illusion, building their houses on sand.

There are those who believe that these *Yamas* and *Niyamas* are outfashioned, and too difficult to be practised in the modern world. There are false teachers who teach that *Yama* and *Niyama* may not be taken so seriously. Such people have never testified the laws in their life and they will be soon swept by the storm of diseases. To climb the mountain we must begin at the bottom, and the *Yama* and *Niyama* are the first steps that lead us to the top. What is required is an iota of practice, if we are serious and sincere. This will transform us from being what we are right now, to being common, ordinary, simple, honest and truthful. This eradicates many evils and diseases that confront man today. Let us stop speculating, which is the most dangerous of all diseases. Let us lead a life that is simple, truthful and honest.

5

SPIRITUAL VALUE OF YAMA

Every structure has its foundation. Every temple has its pillars. So also spiritual life which stands on its ethical foundation. Ethical life is a preparation for spiritual life. The continuous practice and observance of ethical life is a must for the *sādhaka* who seeks the knowledge of the Higher Spiritual life. Spiritual life not based on ethical foundation crumbles and collapses. It itself is inclusive of moral life. If spiritual life is one side of the coin the other side is moral life. Such is the inalienable relationship between the two. Each religion has its own moral code for its practitioners. But, it is a known fact that it is rarely observed by the members. The moral code laid down in yoga is unique; it arises from *Yama* and *Niyama*, the first two limbs of *Astānga Yoga*. These two are like two pillars of yogic life laid down by Patanjali, on which the life of higher yoga which starts with *Dhārana*, and moves upto *Samādhi* through *dhyāna* stands. So, if the *sādhaka* wants to reach this higher yoga he has to undergo certain physical and mental discipline. The purpose of moral code expounded in the *Yoga Sūtras* has this connotation, on which

Patanjali does not make any compromise.

The five cardinal virtues of *Yama* are *Ahimsā, Satya, Āsteya, Brahmacharya* and *Aparigraha (Ahimsā-Satyāsteya-brahmacharyāparigraha Yamah, Sādhana Pāda: Sūtra* 30).[1] The main object of these virtues is to prevent *sādhaka* from doing negative thinking and action. The significant result of practising these five moral qualities is given in five *Sūtras*: 35, 36, 37, 38 and 39. While considering the significance of each of these virtues, the result will also be discussed as provided in the *Sūtras*.

The first of these is *Ahimsā*, a combination of two Sanskrit words a+himsā (अ+हिंसा). *Himsā* is violence, 'a' (अ) stands for 'not'. It is opposite of violence, that is, non-violence. In spiritual life it has a greater implication. It cannot be used in a restricted sense, which means that principle of non-violence cannot be applied only to human beings, but to the whole of creation. This is one sense. Another meaning is that *himsā* need not be explicitly demonstrated. Even before it is seen in the form of action, *himsā* takes place in the form of thought. It is the thought that precedes action. Hence, thought is given greater stress. In fact, *himsā* really denotes an attitude and mode of behaviour towards all living creatures based on the recognition of the underlying principle of unity of life. Yogic philosophy is based on the fundamental doctrine of 'One life'. What flows in each of us and the other creatures is life (*prāna*). It is this principle of life that is common to all creation. In the cosmic creation, every creature

---

[1]अहिंसासत्यास्तेयब्रह्मचर्यापरिग्रह यमः। *Sādhana Pāda, Sūtra* 30.

and inanimate thing has its own significance and plays its part in relation to the whole. If we understand this truth thoroughly we will not harm anything either by thought or action. The *sādhaka* is then blessed, and love springs from this virtue. The specific effect of this virtue is described in *Sūtra* 35 of *Sādhana Pāda* (*Ahimsā-pratisthāyāmtat-samnidhau vairatyāgah*).[2] The *sādhaka* who has developed *ahimsa* is free from any hostility. *Vairatyāga* means abandonment of hostility. What takes place in it is boundless love and compassion, even though this may not be expressed at the emotional level. So the *sādhaka* has to keep an utmost vigilance over his mind, emotions, words and actions. There is no other way. Gradually, when he perfects his thoughts, emotions and actions, he will emerge and transform himself into the positive and dynamic life of love and compassion and service.

The second moral quality is *Satya.* This too has to be taken in a far more comprehensive sense than mere truthfulness. It means abjuring all pretensions, hypocrisy, equivocations, and exaggerations. The opposite is *asatya,* untruthfulness which creates all kinds of unnecessary complications in life and disturbances (*viksepas*) which again prevent the *sādhaka* from concentrating on the higher spiritual life. He shall not progress. On the contrary, it leads to self-ruination. The severity of this virtue is such that the *sādhaka* cannot and must not deviate from the truth. Any slight deviation or an utterance of a lie will forfeit all his hitherto made efforts to pursue

---

[2]अहिंसाप्रतिष्ठायां तत्संनिधौ वैरत्यागः । *Sādhana Pāda, Sūtra* 35.

his spiritual life. This subtler level of practice is unknown to an untruthful man. This is revealed only to a sincere practitioner. It is said a person who starts practising yoga without first acquiring mastery over truthfulness is like a man sailing a river in a boat without rudder. Such is the power of *satya mārga.*

The fruit of this virtue is described in *Sūtra* 36 of *Sādhana Pāda* as *Satya pratisthāyām kriyā-phalāsrayatvam.*[3] The meaning of this *Sūtra* is that the *sādhaka* who has been firmly established in truthfulness will reap the fruit of any action unfailingly. His utterance will become a reality. However, the meaning cannot be pushed to the logical but absurd conclusion of anything getting materialized if a man of truthfulness utters. What it means in reality is that a truthful man will have a greater perspective and understanding of things in nature and that in his own actions he will not try to utter anything that is detrimental to the creation itself. Such a man's mind is purified and highly developed and it can reflect the whole universe in which the past, present and future can be seen to a great extent. It is this reflection of the Divine that makes the *sādhaka* remarkable and whatever he says will come true, and whatever he attempts to accomplish will be accomplished. As the *sādhaka* himself becomes the Divine in the long run of his adherence to truth, and the Divine in turn dwells in such a person, he will not do anything that upsets the order. Even if he does so, it is self-destructive.

[3]सत्यप्रतिष्ठायां क्रियाफलाश्रयत्वम्। *Sādhana Pāda, Sūtra* 36.

But this can never happen as the *sādhaka* is extremely vigilant and weighs every word before he utters and action before he performs. Carelessness is anathema to him.

The next virtue in *Yama* is *Āsteya* which means abstaining from stealing. This word too must be taken in a very comprehensive sense and not in a narrow sense. It should not be viewed only in the sense of abstaining from stealing any object or article that does not belong to one's own. But it should be interpreted as misappropriation of all kinds. The *sādhaka* is forbidden from possessing anything that does not belong to him. At the same time this virtue also demands on the part of the *sādhaka* that he should not possess more than what he requires for his basic needs because the excess or the unnecessary causes *viksepa,* thereby he cannot proceed further in his higher spiritual pursuits. The effect of this moral quality is given in Sūtra 37 of the *Sādhana Pāda* (*Āsteya-pratisthāyām sarva-ratnopasthānam*).[4] The *Sūtra* explains that on being firmly established in honesty all kinds of gems (*ratna*) are given (*upasthānam*) to the yogi. Here gems should be viewed as benefits or treasures of all kinds relating to pure, tranquil state which is imperative for the *sādhaka* to have *dhyāna.* As long as the *sādhaka* has the tendency to misappropriate or covet things which do not belong to him, fresh *karmas* arise and possess him. Once again he will be caught in the mess of life. The power of this moral quality is such that the *sādhaka* as he practises it in true

[4]आस्तेयप्रतिष्ठायां सर्वरत्नोपस्थानम्। *Sādhana Pāda, Sūtra* 37.

spirit will in course of time attract people who may pour their wealth of all kinds. But in true sincerity to the yogic life, the *sādhaka* should remain unattached, he should not claim as his own. Here again, he should be extremely watchful of his tendencies. Suddenly the remnants of the past tendencies (*vāsanās*) may spring forth and there is every chance of his being caught in their snares. A complete obliteration of these undesirable tendencies until their last traces have been removed is required. Hence, the *sādhaka* should persist in his practice with greater cognizance.

Of all the virtues of *Yama*, *Brahmacharya* is most important for the *sādhaka* if he wants to tread the higher spiritual life. This word too has been misinterpreted in several ways not knowing its true significance in spiritual parlour. Patanjali does not compromise on the vagaries of *Brahmacharya*. The *sādhaka* can never have two things at a time, aspiring for the higher spiritual life while keeping another leg in indulgences. This is strictly forbidden. The *sādhaka* has to choose between the two before he really embarks upon his higher yogic life. So, the first thing that the *sādhaka* must understand is that for the higher yoga he should completely abstain from sex life and no compromise on this point is possible. Second, if he has seriously decided to pursue the higher yogic life, he should systematically train himself in desisting from even thoughts and emotions connected with the pleasures of sex. An implication is that abstinence is not merely related to the sex life, but anything that is sensual enjoyment. The sensual pleasures need not necessarily be associated with sex life but they may even be related to objects and things. The contact with the objects/things and the deep attachment to them will create *samskāras* which act like *viksepas* in the *sādhaka*. So, a severe self-discipline coupled with an austere life is essential for the *sādhaka*. Many doubt and wonder as to what benefits would yield for a yogi, and how a complete renunciation of sexual life and leading an austere life would have any worth for him. The benefit accrued is described in *Sūtra* 38 of the *Sādhana Pāda* as *Brahmacharya-pratisthāyām vīrya-lābhah*[5] which means in literal translation as "on being firmly established in sexual continence vigour is gained". *Vīrya* here stands for vitality which makes all parts of body vibrant and vigorous. When sexual energy is sublimated, it is converted into spiritual energy, which is called *ojas*. This energy approximately resembles cosmic energy which is pure and subtle. The *sādhaka* thereby gains extraordinary resilience, strength and energy. It is this energy that acts like an aura, which constantly protects the *sādhaka* as long as he treads the path of *Brahmacharya*. The moment the *sādhaka* slackens in the treading of the higher path, the aura disappears. Thereafter, whatever the amount of practice that he may do, it will not result in a positive way. This conservation and transmutation of sexual energy is acquired not merely by abstention from the sex but by a very strict and rigid control of sexual thoughts and desires. *Brahmacharya*, therefore, is comprehensive which forbids the *sādhaka* from experiencing anything that is sensual either mentally

[5]ब्रह्मचर्यप्रतिष्ठायां वीर्यलाभः । *Sādhana Pāda, Sūtra* 38.

or physically. It is only under severity of this discipline that the *sādhaka* can sublimate the grosser energy to serve the higher purposes of spiritual life. If this discipline is cultivated at an early age, it is better.

The last moral virtue in *Yama* is *Aparigraha* which means not only the absence of greediness but also non-possessiveness. The tendency to accumulate at the cost of the peril of society is strong amongst us. Similarly, the tendency to possess that which is not ours is also a sin. In yogic life it is an obstacle. It is true we need certain things for our daily living. To make our life more comfortable we keep adding more and more luxuries and in course of time we get so attached to them that we go mad when such comforts are removed from our life. One might argue here that these are basic necessities and essential. But the question what is essential and what is not essential is a matter of mental taste and maintenance of the body and there seems to be no limit to the cutting down of even what are considered the necessities of life. So, there is no end to our satisfaction. In yogic life there is no compromise on this. The *sādhaka* must give up all temptations and be prepared to undergo any kind of hostile life. First of all, he should put an end to the liking for comfortability. He should attain the sense of equanimity in all situations irrespective of their nature. This is an essential condition for the *sādhaka* to tread the higher path. He should be able to learn to live the simple and austere life. There is no other way to perfect *aparigraha.*

Its effect is mentioned in Sūtra 39 of the *Sādhana Pāda* as *Aparigraha-Sthairyejanma-kathamtā-sambodhah*[6] which means that when non-possessiveness becomes steadfast, there arises knowledge of the 'how' and 'wherefor' of existence. Attachment and anxiety which accompany it are obstacles to knowledge. Non-attachment takes us to the higher levels of knowledge which percolates down into our lower consciousness. It makes us see all our past knowledge and enables us to understand how we came into this world and what for. This knowledge further strengthens the confidence of the *sādhaka* who may proceed further in his pursuits with greater perseverance and intelligence.

The purpose of these five cardinal virtues of *Yama* is to eliminate completely all mental and emotional disturbances so that the *sādhaka* can stabilize himself in his higher pursuits of yoga. It should be noted here that no freedom from emotional and mental disturbances is possible until the negative tendencies dealt with under the five *Yamas* are completely rooted out. So long as these negative tendencies persist in the *sādhaka* either in their gross form or in subtle form which affect the mind, it is pointless to undertake the journey in the higher yoga.

---

[6]अपरिग्रहस्थैर्ये जन्मकथंतासंबोधः । *Sādhana Pāda, Sūtra* 39.

6
SPIRITUAL VALUE OF NIYAMA

We now come to the second *anga* of yoga discipline, the five 'dos' of *Niyama*. They are *Saucha-Samtōsa-Tapah-Svādhyāyesvara-Pranidhānāni* (*Sūtra* 32, *Sādhana Pāda*).[1] The virtues included in *Yama* are moral, instructive and prohibitive in nature, while those in *Niyama* are constructive and positive. The former lays the ethical foundation the latter prepares the *sādhaka* for the higher yogic life. However, these two are not mutually exclusive. They are complementary to each other. They are the two sides of the same coin. Both are imperative for the *sādhaka* to tread the yogic life. Both are like two legs of the yogic life. One without the other makes the *sādhaka* lame. For proper pursuing of the yogic life both are obligatory.

Now let us consider each virtue and its effect. The first element of *Niyama* is *saucha*, which is purity. It is a complex word. What is purity? It should not be viewed segmentwise. It is, on the other, to be understood in its totality. That is, purity not only in body but also in mind. Both are integral parts of

[1]शौचसंतोषतपः स्वाध्यायेश्वरप्रणिधानानि। *Sādhana Pāda, Sūtra* 32.

human being. Both have mutual impact on each other. If the body goes wrong, the mind cannot concentrate. If the mind goes wrong the body gets affected.

First, let us take purity of body which is generally neglected in yogic life. Unless body is made a fitting vehicle, spiritual *sādhana* is impossible. Each cell has to be purified by eliminating the toxic elements which make the body coarse and unfit. As long as these toxic elements are present, body is more prone to diseases. With the diseased body the *sādhaka* cannot take up yoga. Hence, it is to be made resilient and it may be brought about by supplying the right kind of food which should be highly *sāttvic* in quality. A strong adherence to this food will in course of time make the body sufficiently refined.

Second, purity must also be aimed at the mental level. How is purity achieved at the mind level? Mind at a subtler level expresses itself in the form of thoughts and emotions. These have to be purified. Generally, we are filled with negative thoughts and emotions knowing that they are pretty harmful. We continue to live in them and with them, without which, in most situations, we go mad. Unless these negative thoughts and emotions are eliminated completely purity has no meaning. These cause great *viksepas* and the *sādhaka* cannot proceed on to the other *angas* of yoga. A pure mind is like mirror without stain which can reflect the sun-like truth. Such a mind, when once it is attained, cannot again fall prey to negative thoughts and emotions. It guards itself on its own. A pure mind naturally thinks of pure thoughts and feels pure emotions. A constant vigilance coupled with strong determination and will power will check the undesirable thoughts and emotions. Further, it should be noted here that this pure mind should be attained here and now and at once, and it should not be for a day or a few days. The *sādhaka* has to go through purificatory exercises every moment.

The results of developing purity are given in *Sūtras* 40 and 41 of *Samādhi Pāda. Sūtra* 40 says: *Saucāt svānga-jugupsā parair asamsargah.*[2] This *Sūtra* relates to the effect of purity of body. As a result of purity, there arises disgust for one's own body and indifference to physical contact with others. Why does one develop disgust towards body? It arises out of understanding the fact that this body is only a mass and it slowly degenerates and finally perishes. So, it has no permanency. If this is realized one will not give too much importance to it, which again should not be construed that this body should be neglected. Body is required, but its perishable nature does not make one attach oneself to it. Besides, after purification the body is made so sensitive that it makes see things as they really are. The second result is naturally a corollary to the first one. A person who feels disgust for his own body will not develop any attraction towards other bodies which are tainted and unclean. This does not mean that he develops hatred which goes against the principle of love. It only means that he becomes sensitive to those bodies which are comparatively less clean.

---

[2]शौचात् स्वाङ्गजुगुप्सा परैरसंसर्गः । *Sādhana Pāda, Sūtra* 40.

Sūtra 41 relates to the result of purity of mind. The *Sūtra* reads as *Sattvasuddhi-saumanasyaikāgryendriya-jayātma-darsana-yogyatvāni.*[3] It means that from the purity of mind arises the four results, cheerfulness of mind, one-pointedness, control of the passions and fitness for the vision of the Higher self. The purity of mind gives *Sattva guna* which alone can enable the mind to reflect upon Higher consciousness. This purification (*Sattva suddhi*) is fundamental for concentration (*dhārana*), meditation (*dhyāna*) and *Samādhi.* It should also be seen that *Sattva suddhi* is fundamental and the other consequences specified in the *Sūtra* are natural. If the mind is in its usual course, given to all kinds of emotions and feelings and thoughts, it causes *viksepa.* A disturbed and disintegrated mind is certainly unfit for achieving the higher goals in yoga.

The second element of *Niyama* is *Santōsa* which is equivalent to contentment. Contentment has spiritual connotation, whereas satisfaction is purely mundane. Satisfaction multiples itself, it breeds into endless satisfaction. While in contentment, there is no further craving, it implies an acceptance of life as it is given. It is necessary for the *sādhaka* to cultivate contentment of the highest order because without it there is no possibility of keeping the mind in equilibrium. Running after things results in *viksepa.*

The effect of this quality is presented in *Sūtra* 42 which reads as *Samtosād anuttamah sukha-lābhah.*[4]

---

[3]सत्त्वशुद्धिसौमनस्यैकाग्र्येन्द्रियजयात्मदर्शनयोग्यत्वानि । *Sādhana Pāda, Sūtra* 41.

[4]संतोषादनुत्तमः सुखलाभः । *Sādhana Pāda, Sūtra* 42.

As the result of contentment (*santōsa*) one gains supreme happiness (*sukha lābhah*). This is quite natural. The chief cause of unhappiness is entertaining all kinds of desires and trying to fulfil them by hook or crook without caring for their serious negative consequences. Unless these desires not only in conscious mind but also in subconscious mind are eliminated, restlessness persists. Real and perfect happiness comes into effect when we have contentment with what we have. The mind acquires crystal clarity and silken pond-like tranquillity. It is only in that state does true happiness lie.

Tapas is the next element in *Niyama*. It is a comprehensive term. It combines in itself purification, self-discipline and austerity. A general tendency prevailing among certain schools interprets this term in the strict extreme sense such as this term in the mortifying the body through vigorous fasting. This is highly reprehensible to the spirit of yoga. By self-mortification nothing can be achieved. What is to be aimed at is to eliminate all those that cause *viksepa* at the lower level. This involves a process of following a life of simplicity, contentment, honesty, and truthfulness. What is to be achieved finally is to destroy the petty ego. It is only when this is acquired the *sādhaka* can effectively put himself on the track of higher yoga.

The result of the practice of this virtue is stated in *Sūtra* 43 of the *Sādhana Pāda* which reads as *kāyendriya-siddhir asuddhi-ksayāt tapasah.*[5] In literal translation it means that by *tapas* impurities are

---

[5] कायेन्द्रियसिद्धिरशुद्धिक्षयात् तपसः। *Sādhana Pāda, Sūtra* 43.

removed, thereby we acquire *siddhis*. The word *siddhi* can be understood in two senses—both in the sense of occult power and perfection. Though the *sādhaka* gains occult powers such as the power of clairvoyance, clairaudience, telepathy, levitation, etc. in course of time they are incidental and such should be viewed as happening in the transition stage of spiritual life. The ultimate goal of *tapas* is to bring in perfection. The perfection comes when *Asuddhi-ksayāt* is performed. The main purpose of *tapas* is to remove impurities and attain perfection. That is, when the whole system is purified it can function perfectly as an instrument of consciousness.

The fourth *Niyama* is *Svādhyāya* which means the study of self which leads to knowledge. The study of self can come both from outside and inside. Reading scriptures, other important texts which contain immense spiritual values and gospels of great teachers is part of study that comes from outside. Though this constitutes as the first step, it is not the last step. It is only a beginning for the *sādhaka* who has to acquaint himself with all the spiritual processes in theory. While this study is only theoretical and does not take him deep into the spiritual life, the next step therefore is to ponder and reflect deeply on the ideas and thoughts. This is very essential for the *sādhaka* as without proper reflecting upon life, any reading of scriptural literatures becomes meaningless. For this a broad and general intellectual background is necessary. This constant reflection prepares the mind for the reception of real knowledge from within. This study constitutes knowledge from within. This brooding and reflecting on the fundamental truths of life gradually leads the *sādhaka* to meditation. So, it is seen that *svādhyāya* involves two-way process—the study from without and the study from within. Both are essential, and complementary to each other, the one should lead to the other progressively and finally to *Dhyāna*. That is the significance of *sva* meaning 'self' and *adhyāya* meaning 'study'. Books should act like external aids, but in the process, the *sādhaka* should rely more on himself for understanding the mysteries of life and greater knowledge.

The benefit is discussed in *Sūtra* 44 of *Sādhana Pāda* which reads as *svādhyāyād ista-devatā-samprayōgah.*[6] By self-study one obtains union (*samprayōgah*) with the vision of God (*Ista devatā*) which the *sādhaka* has chosen. This is the final acme in *Svādhyāya* because this is the ultimate purpose, and the final goal of yogic life. All other pursuits without attaining this goal become pointless. In the process a patient waiting is required. The *sādhaka* should not aim at these benefits. Instead, he should strive hard, without expecting any results. But, if one is serious, it gradually leads him to the Ultimate. When this communion is achieved, there arises free flow of knowledge and understanding from the Higher.

The last virtue in *Niyama* is *Īshvara-pranidhāna*, which stands for resignation to God or self-surrender. For the *sādhaka* ultimately this is essential, a complete resignation to the ultimate power as this will increase his faith. In this complete surrender, there is no clinging to the body or any material

---

[6]स्वाध्यायादिष्टदेवतासंप्रयोगः । *Sādhana Pāda, Sūtra* 44.

(*padārtha*) which has the *guna* of changing and perishing. He should have a complete mental assertion that the will of the Ultimate Power is supreme in the whole creation and to that will he should submit himself unswervingly. The *īshvara pranidhāna* in *bhakti* literature is known as *prapatti* or *saranāgati*. The doctrine of *prapatti* is strong in *bhakti yoga* as it alone increases the devotion, and leads the *bhakta* to the final communion with the Supreme power by means of love. Here it is love which is the driving force. In *īshvara pranidhāna* the will is the driving force. It is surrendered to the Divine will. Also, it serves as a means by which the *asmita* (I-ness) is removed. As there is a complete surrender to the Supreme power, the 'I'-ness will be replaced by the Supreme will, and all thoughts and actions thereafter are done in that will. Individual will is replaced by the Divine will, but it does not end there. The real process of spiritualization has begun and the *sādhaka* has to proceed further in his *nirantara sādhana* for the ultimate dissolution which takes place only when *Samādhi* is realized. Such a *sādhaka* does actions in the pure *nishkāma* sense. Whether one really achieves the realization of the divine in *īshvara pranidhāna* is questionable. What happens in the assumption in true sense is that it acts as a means for climbing up the higher ladder of spiritual life.

Patanjali discusses the effect of this virtue in *Sūtra* 45 as *Samādhi-siddhir īshvara-pranidhānāt*.[7] Resignation to God leads to *Samādhi*. By this

---

[7]समाधिसिद्धिरीश्वरप्रणिधानात्। *Sādhana Pāda, Sūtra* 45.

advantage, Patanjali has given a unique status to *Īshvara Pranidhāna*. He hasn't given such an independent status to any virtue. The attainment of *Samādhi* through *īshvara pranidhāna* is a startling and remarkable revelation. It is because it develops *para vairāgya* in the *sādhaka* which eliminates *Asmita* ('I'-ness). When this 'I'-ness is removed *Vrittīs* (modifications) are automatically controlled and obliterated. Then *citta* becomes pure. It is this purity that unfolds divine consciousness which is temporarily concealed by *vrittīs* and *asmita.*

Thus, we see from the preceding paragraphs that the five *Niyamas* stress the positive aspect of life. They tell us what we should do in order to heighten our pursuit of Higher spiritual life and reach the goal. The five virtues of *Yama* and the five virtues of *Niyama* have high spiritual value. If one observes them in true spirit, gradually he realizes the presence of Divine consciousness. Divine is pure. Purity comes into contact with purity and stays in it. It does not go with impurities. The purpose of *Yama* and *Niyama* is to eliminate these impurities in us so that we get more and more purified. This purification is nothing but becoming subtle. As we become subtle, Divine consciousness expresses itself more and more. Water flows only into shallow places. So also divine consciousness flows into lower levels of our consciousness when purified.

7

STHIRA SUKHAM ĀSANAM

Āsanam is the third important limb in *Astānga Yoga* which later came to be identified with physical development. But Patanjali nowhere in his *Yoga Sūtras* discusses the physical development in the truest *Hatha Yoga* sense. For Patanjali *āsana* is only a means and preparation for *dhyāna.* He has not prescribed any elaborate *āsanas* to be performed by a *sādhaka.* Only in three *Sūtras* (46, 47 and 48 in *Sādhana Pāda*) he refers to *āsana.* Here, Patanjali differs from other schools of yoga that came later and emphasised *Hatha Yoga.*

In fact, many people who do not know anything about Patanjali's yoga, confuse it with these physical exercises. The place and purpose of *āsana* in Patanjali's *Astānga Yoga* is different from the purpose as it is known in *Hatha Yoga.* Patanjali's yoga is known as *Rāja Yoga;* consequently its purpose is limited only to prepare oneself for *dhyāna* for which a stabilised posture is essential.

In *Hatha Yoga* the subject of *āsana* is treated at great length. *Hatha Yoga* is based on the principle that changes in consciousness can be brought about by setting in motion currents of certain kinds of subtler forces (*Prāna, Kundalini*) in the physical body. The first requirement is to make the physical body perfectly healthy and fit for the influx and manifestation of these forces. It is for this reason a strong emphasis is laid on *āsanas* and the *sādhaka* is required to go through different kinds of *āsanas* which are dealt with in treatises on *Hatha-Yoga*.

The so-called modern *Hatha Yoga* is limited to the name of Gorakhanatha, the founder of the Order of Kanphata Yogis. Historically he was placed in the 12th century AD. He is said to have written a treatise entitled *Hatha Yoga* and also a preserved text which goes by the name *Goraksasataka.* The first treatise on *Hatha Yoga* is said to have been lost. Apart from this, the three most well known Hatha Yoga 'classics' are: *Hatha Yoga-Pradīpikā* of Svatmarana Swami (probably belonged to 15th century AD), *Siva-Samhita,* and *Gheranda Samhita.* Of these three, *Siva Samhita* is considered the longest and slightly more philosophical in its approach. It is somewhat coloured by the Vedanta school. The author of *Gheranda Samhita* is not known. It is in the form of a dialogue between Gheranda, the preceptor and Candakapali, the disciple. Whether these two names are real or fictitious is not definitely known. However, it is assumed, based on certain contents in the text which refer to a considerable influence of Vaisnavism on the author, that the author was an adept named Gheranda—a Vaisnavite of Bengal. Whatever the arguments about its original author may be, the text widely differs from *Hatha Yoga Pradīpikā* and other texts on *Hatha Yoga.* It does not use the word *Hatha* in the form of yoga, but only in the sense of 'force'. The yoga that is discussed in the text is called *Ghatastha Yoga.* 'Ghata' refers to body and *Ghatastha Yoga* means yoga based on the approach through the body. Obviously *Ghatastha Yoga* or *Ghata Yoga* deals with the *Hatha Yogic* practices. Unlike Patanjali's *Astānga Yoga* this yoga is known as *Saptānga Yoga*—sevenfold yoga, which includes *Satkarmas, Āsanas, Mudrās, Pratyāhāra, Prānāyāma, Dhyāna* and *Samādhi.*

Āsanas are described in all the three texts. The *Gheranda Samhita* mentions 32 *āsanas*; *Hatha Yoga Pradīpikā* describes 14; the *Yoga Pradīpikā*, 21; the *Visva-Kōsa,* 32; and the *Anubhava Prakāsa,* 50. However, they all seem to agree that the total number of postures is 84. Four of these postures are vey generally practised and favoured by yogins: *Siddhāsana, Padmāsana, Svastikāsana* and *Simhāsana.* Patanjali does not discuss any of the 84 *āsanas* in his treatise *Yoga Sūtras.* He gives only the three *sūtras* regarding the technique of *āsanās.* The first of these is *Sthira-Sukham Āsanam* (*Sādhana Pāda, Sūtra* 46)[1] which means posture should be steady and comfortable. The Sūtra has two important words, *sthira* and *sukha. Sthira* means steadiness, without any movement in the body. It does not mean to have a considerable freedom to move the parts of body, or to make adjustments from time to time. It means fixing the body in a particular position for a longer time. Steadiness is not for a few minutes, but should be achieved for a longer time, say for thirty minutes

---

[1]स्थिरसुखमासनम्। *Sādhana Pāda, Sūtra* 46.

minimum and maximum time is left to the practitioner's capacity.

Another key word is *sukha* which means comfortable. It is not enough to remain in one position for a longer time but it should be a comfortable one. The body should be in a total relaxed condition. There should not be any rigidity which makes the body tense. This will have adverse effect not only on the health of body but also on *Dhyāna.* The whole posture should be in a complete relaxed state. It is only then can the *sādhaka* meditate. So, in the next *Sūtra* (47) of *Sādhanapāda* it is stated: *Prayatna-Saithilyānanta-Samāpattibhyām.*[2] By relaxation and meditation on the *ananta* (endless) the posture is mastered. For acquiring mastery of an *āsana* Patanjali gives two useful suggestions. One is the gradual slackening of effort. In the beginning effort is required. Here, effort means directing the mind on the body whenever the latter becomes unsteady. This again makes the mind unsteady as it keeps now and then directing the body in order to maintain it in the fixed position. This state is not conducive for *dhyāna,* which becomes possible only when the mind is released from the consciousness of the body. So the *sādhaka* is advised to slacken the effort gradually and facilitate himself in such a way as to direct the mind withdraw from the consciousness of the body without affecting its fixed condition. This is a gradual process, suggested in the *Sūtra,* which involves a definite effort in the beginning and later becomes effortless.

---

[2]प्रयत्नशैथिल्यानन्तसमापत्तिभ्याम्। *Sādhana Pāda, Sūtra* 47.

The other means recommended in the *Sūtra* for acquiring the steadiness is meditation on the *ananta*, which may be viewed as the Great Power that envelops the whole cosmos. This might suggest obscurity for the *sādhaka*. Therefore, in such condition when the *sādhaka* fails to imagine or visualise the Great Power he can direct this power to a particular deity which in turn may become a symbolic representation of that power, and later he can direct his mind-consciousness on it, thus slacken his control on the body. In this way he can prepare himself for *Dhyāna*. Ultimately, from the discussion of the two *sūtras* it is understood that *āsana* means forgetting about the consciousness of body, and fusing the mind with the *ananta* known as *Samāpattibhyām*.

In the third *Sūtra* the most important result of attaining perfection in the practice of *āsana* is mentioned. It reads as: *Tato dvandvānabhighātah* (*Sādhana Pāda*, Sūtra 48).[3] It means that from the practice of *āsana* the *sādhaka* is no longer troubled by the dualities of the phenomenal world. These *dvandvas* (dualities) relating to the body and mind may produce *viksepa* or distraction in the *sādhaka* whose meditation may be affected. One important result of gaining perfection in the practice of *āsana* is freedom from these *viksepas*. Apart from this result mentioned by Patanjali, there are other important benefits which accrue from this practice of *āsana*. They are: (i) The *sādhaka* gains the power of concentration, consequently, his memory will be increased manifold; (ii) The *sādhaka* may acquire fitness for doing *Prānāyāma*; (iii) The *sādhaka* can

---

[3]ततो द्वन्द्वानभिघातः । *Sādhana Pāda, Sūtra* 48.

develop strong will power, both mental and spiritual. This will power in turn makes the *sādhaka* face the challenges of life boldly and at the same time prepares him to aspire for higher spiritual experiences.

Finally, we come to the question which *āsana* the *sādhaka* has to choose for the practice of *dhyāna.* Here, there is no hard and fast rule. The *sādhaka* can choose any *āsana* which suits his body composition. Generally, for *dhyāna,* either *Padmāsana* or *Siddhāsana* is recommended. But, for those who find it difficult are advised to go in for *Sukhāsana* or *Ardha Padmāsana.* After choosing the one the *sādhaka* should practise remaining in that posture for longer times until he/she gains mastery in it. If the *āsana* is chosen and practised correctly, the *sādhaka* can overcome all the minor discomforts and distractions that he/she may encounter in the initial stage. Thereafter, his success in *dhyāna* becomes easier and less arduous. Stabilisation in particular posture is an essential requirement for *dhyāna.* This steadiness checks all the distracted thought flow and prepares it for the free flow of pranic force in the body, from the *mūlādhāra chakra* to *āgna chakra.* If the flow is steady and even, the gates of *samādhi* are opened and the *sādhaka* can enter it without any tremor. After considerable practice, for the *sādhaka* the steadiness of mind becomes a natural process. Even *samādhi* happens naturally without any volition on his part. Such *samādhi* obtained naturally without effort is called *sahaja samādhi.* It is a long way to go for that. But patience and perseverance, the twin virtues, are required to achieve this desirable result.

8
PRĀNĀYĀMA

Patanjali deals with *Prānāyāma* in five *Sūtras* (49, 50, 51, 52, & 53) in *Sādhana Pāda* of *Yoga Sūtras*. However, his method of *Prānāyāma* is different from the way it has been elaborately dealt with in *Hatha Yoga Pradīpikā*. In Hatha Yoga, *Prānāyāma* is used to manipulate the pranic currents so as to bring change in consciousness. In *Gheranda Samhita* it is central to Yoga. Gheranda deals with the question of time and place and regulated nourishment, the purification of *Nādis*, the various *prānas* and the eightfold *prānāyāma*: Sahita, Suryabheda, Ujjayi, Sitali, Bhastrika, Bhramari, Murcha and Kevali.

Importance of Prānāyāma

The importance of *Prānāyāma* in the practice of Yoga is highly stressed. It is written in *Hatha Yoga Pradīpikā* as: "The mind is the master of the senses; the life-breath is the master of the mind; the master of the life-breath is its absorption. The absorption of the mind is achieved by (listening to) the inner sound" (*Indriyarāga mano nātho manonāthastu mastah mastasyah layo nāthah sa layo nāthah mākshitah*).[1] The *Siva Samhita* also extols its virtues: "The master of Yoga, through breath-control, acquires the eight superhuman powers. He crosses beyond the ocean of sin and virtue and freely wanders in the three worlds" (*Prāragayamena Yogīndro labdha vaisvayastikāni va pāpa punyodadhi teertvā trailokya charatāmiyāt*).[2] Sankaracharya in his commentary on *Svetasvatara Upanishad* praises *Prānāyāma*: "The soul purified by Prānāyāma realizes the Supreme Spirit (*Parabrahman*). Hence, according to Supreme Revelation, the *Sruti*, there is nothing superior to *Prānāyāma*." In the words of Yajnavalkya Samhita: "All become liberated verily by the control of *Prāna*. They all attain salvation who get purified by *Prānāyāma*. The control of *prāna*, truly, is the vessel that carries the afflicted across the ocean of manifestation to Liberation." For *Yogachintamani* the position is clear: "The processes of *Pratyāhāra*, *Dhārana*, *Dhyāna* and *Samādhi* are truly *Prānāyāma* gradually increasing in the practice." Gheranda in his *Gheranda Samhitā* gives us the twin purpose of *Prānāyāma*: entire harmony and complete mental control. He says that it is only to control the fickle mind that intelligent yogins perform *Prānāyāma*.

What is Prāna?

Let us first know what *Prāna* is before we attempt to examine what Patanjali has said about it. *Prāna* is the universal principle of energy or force. It is very

---

[1]इन्द्रियरागा मनो नाथो मनोनाथस्तुमस्त: ।
मस्तस्य: लयो नाथ: स लयो नाथ: माक्षित: ॥

[2]प्रारगयमेन योगीन्द्रो लब्धवैश्वयष्टिकानि व ।
पापपुण्योदधि तीर्त्वा त्रैलोक्यचरताम्यियात् ॥

subtle and invisible. It is vital force. It is called the universal life-force. It is all-pervading. It is the link between the astral body and the physical body. When this is cut off, the astral body separates from the physical body and death takes place. This *prāna* remained in a subtle, motionless, unmanifested, undifferentiated state in the beginning of Creation. When the manifestation took place, it vibrated and moved in all directions. Now, this manifestation is ever continuing and ever expressing and ever expanding. So *Prāna* is in continuous manifestation and expansion. It is found in all forms. Where there is *prāna*, there is *Chalana* (movement) and action. It is the *prāna* that performs every kind of function in any organism. All physical forces and mental forces become active because of the presence of *prāna*. Hatha Yogis consider it superior to mind-principle because it is a force that activates the latter. Hence, for them *prāna* plays a more vital role than the mind. When the seminal energy is sublimated, or transformed, it becomes 'Ojas' which is nothing but *prāna*. It is stored up in each and every cell of body and a yogi will never dissipate it unnecessarily. He stores it up by regular practice of *Prānāyāma*. Scriptures identify *prāna* with *Brahman*.

Prāna is not vague and mysterious; it is real. It is a kind of composite energy with a material basis which is different from the other kinds of energies working in the body. The vehicle of the *prāna* is not the dense physical body but the *prānamaya kosa* a subtler vehicle interpenetrating the dense physical body and working in conjunction with it.

Prāna and its Various Functions

Though *Prāna* is one, it assumes different forms with different functions. The five most important functions are: *prāna, apāna, samāna, udāna* and *vyāna.* Of these the *prāna* and *apāna* are important agents. Each has its own seat in the human body and each has its own functions. The seat of *prāna* is the heart and it works in the regions like facial, nostrils, navel and the heart. It is the cause for sound, utterance and breath. *Apāna* is the arms and it works in the regions of arms, penis, thighs and testicles. It activates these organs and performs the functions of urination, defecation and exertion. The seat of *Samāna* is the navel. It helps digestion and using up of all the energy produced by the food. The seat of *Udāna* is the throat, its action is represented by the joints and the throat. It helps the limbs function in a proper way. While *Vyāna* is all-pervasive, it controls the functions not attended by *prāna* and *apāna.* Each form is represented by a particular colour. Thus, *prāna* is said to be of the colour of blood, red germ or coral, *apāna* of indragopa (an insect of white or red colour), *samāna* of something between *prāna* and *apāna, udāna* of pale white and *vyāna* of a ray of light.

Prāna and Breath

Let us now turn to the differences between breath and *prāna.* Generally, *prāna* is confused with breath and it is often mistaken for *prāna.* Breath is the external manifestation of *prāna.* Breath is gross; *prāna* is subtle. Breath is felt inwardly and outwardly;

whereas the inward presence of *prāna* is the vital principal force which is the cause of existence of body in vibration. By exercising control over the breath one can control the subtle *prāna* inside.

Prāna and Mind

Just as breath and *prāna* are intimately related so also *prāna* and mind. *Prāna* is the connecting link between matter and energy on the one hand and consciousness and mind on the other. Consciousness expressing itself through the mind cannot come into touch with matter and function through it without the intermediate presence of *prāna*. Similarly, matter in association with energy cannot affect consciousness except through the agency of *prāna*. Mind cannot function without *prāna*. It is the vibration of *prāna* that produces thoughts and sets mind in motion. If *prāna* is controlled through certain techniques the mind can also be controlled. The closeness of *Prāna* and mind is such that Sankara claimed in *Aparokshānubhuti* (Verse 118) that "The restraint of all modifications of the mind by regarding all mental states like the *Citta* as Brahman alone, is called *Prānāyāma*."

What is Prānāyāma?

Prānāyāma is the fourth important limb in *Astānga Yoga* propounded by Patanjali. It plays an important role in yogic practice. In Hatha Yoga, *citta vrittīs* are controlled through the manipulation of pranic currents, whereas in Raja Yoga they are controlled by consciousness through the will and *prāna* here comes under the control of the mind. Patanjali has used both the techniques in his system of yoga in order to make it more comprehensive and effective as possible. Thus *prānāyāma* in Patanjali's Yoga System is used as preparation for *Dhārana, Dhyāna* and *Samādhi.*

Prānāyāma is the combination of two words, *prāna,* meaning life-force and *ayama* meaning control. Thus *Prānāyāma* means control of the *prānic* force. It is this which is aimed at in *prānāyāma* and not breathing which is its extension in the physical body. Deep breathing exercises have nothing to do with *prānāyāma.* They may be practised for promoting health. Breathing alternately through the two nostrils may affect the *prānic* currents to a certain extent. It cleanses the congestion in the *nādis* in which *prāna* can flow freely and normally. As such in our body, these *nādis* are filled with toxins, thus affecting the free flow of *prānic* force. Hence, cleansing of these *nādis* is important in the beginning. This is the first step in *Prānāyāma.* This purification of the *nādis* is a preparatory exercise and all those who intend to practise *prānāyāma* have to go through this for a long time. Human body has 72,000 *nādis* of which *Ida, Pingala* and *Sushumna* are important. *Ida* and *Pingala* intertwine the spiritual spinal cord from the anus point and move upward in spiral position and connect each other in the head. *Ida* starts from the right testicle in the *mūlādhāra chakra* and connects it to the left nostril, whereas *pingala* originates from the left testicle and connects it to the right nostril. *Ida* is the seat of coolness, whereas *pingala* the seat of heart. Thus *Ida* represents the moon, *Pingala* the sun. *Sushumna* passes through in the middle. When *Prāna* passes through *Sushumna*, cessation of breathing takes place. Mind enters into a thoughtless state. It is only when this happens, the real spiritual adventure begins. Patanjali says in his *Sūtra* 49 of *Sādhana Pāda* in his treatise *Yoga Sūtras*: *Tasmin sati svāsaprasvāsayor gativicchedah prāṇāyāmah.*[3] This means cessation of in-breathing and out-breathing is *Prāṇāyāma*. When this cessation takes place, *Sushumna* becomes active.

Real *Prāṇāyāma* begins when the breath is stopped between inhalation and exhalation. This period of stop may be increased slowly and gradually. This is technically known as *kumbhaka* (retention). This affects the flow of *prānic* currents in a marked way and it enables the *sādhaka* to gain enough control over them in such a manner that he may use and direct them in any way as he wishes. It is said that the length of air (*vāyu*) that flows in human body is 96 digits (six feet). When exhaled in ordinary way it becomes 12 digits (9 inches), in singing its length will be 16 digits (1 foot), in eating it goes up to 20 digits (15 inches), in sleeping it increases to 30 digits (22.5 inches), in copulation it is further enhanced to 36 digits (27 inches) and in doing physical exercises it is much more. By decreasing the length of the natural exhalation (9 inches) life is prolonged. Slowly when it is achieved to zero level, cessation takes place and the real *prāṇāyāma* takes place.

---

[3]तस्मिन् सति श्वासप्रवासयोर्गतिविच्छेदः प्राणायामः । *Sādhana Pāda, Sūtra* 49.

Two Ways of Prānāyāma

(i) Sahita Kumbhaka Prānāyāma

This *Prānāyāma* (that is, cessation of breathing) can be achieved by the *sādhaka* in two ways. One is with effort and the other without effort. Let us examine the first technique. When *Kumbhaka* is achieved with *puraka* and *rechaka* (inhalation and exhalation), it is called *Sahita Kumbhaka. Kumbhaka* is the essential element in *Prānāyāma.* Patanjali discusses three kinds of *kumbhaka* in *Sūtra* 50 of *Sādhana Pāda: Bāhyābhyantara stambhavrttir desakāla samkhyābhih paridrsto dīrghasūkhanah* (The breath may be stopped externally, internally or suppressed in mid motion, and regulated according to place, time and a fixed number of times, so that the stoppage is prolonged or brief). However, Patanjali does not discuss the techniques by which both internal and external *kumbhaka* is achieved. In Hatha Yoga, the techniques have been presented. A Hatha Yogi unites *prāna* and *apāna* through retention of breath (*kumbhaka*) and this is done by performing *bandhas.* The aim of *Prānāyāma* in Hatha Yoga is to awaken the sleeping *kundalini.* As it awakens, the *sushumna* opens and the united *prāna* and *apāna* is taken through the *sushumna nādi.* The eight kinds of *Prānāyāma* techniques used in Hatha Yoga are: *Surya Bhēda, Ujjayi, Sitakari, Sitali, Bhastrika, Bhramari, Mūrcha* and *Plavini.* The *Bandhas* used are *Mula Bandha, Jalandhara Bandha, Uddiyana Bandha* and *Maha Bandha.*

Bhastrika means bellows. It involves rapid succession of forcible expulsion of air. The inhaling and exhaling are done rapidly like the bellows of the blacksmith. After performing this for ten to fifteen times, then *jalandhara bandha* should be performed in which after sucking the air inside, *kumbhaka* is done by closing the two nostrils by interlocking the chin and the neck. In this *bandha* the *prāna* is united with *apāna* as *Ida* and *Pingala nādis* are shut. This type of *Prānāyāma* has several advantages. It relieves inflammation of the throat, activates gastric fire, removes diseases of the nose and chest and eradicates asthma and bronchitis. It increases appetite and destroys phlegm. It removes all diseases which arise from excess of wind, bile, and phlegm. It works well in winter season because it generates heat in the body and keeps it warm. The practitioner of this *prānāyāma* will never suffer from any disease as it purifies all *nādis.*

Bhramari stands for the humming sound of a bee. In this technique inhaling is done rapidly through both nostrils making the sound of the bee and exhaling too is done rapidly through both nostrils making the humming sound. Later *Jalandhara Bandha* should be performed. In the beginning heat of the body is increased as the circulation of blood is activated. In the end, however, it is decreased by perspiration. In *Mūrcha Prānāyāma* technique after inhaling *kumbhaka* is performed till one feels fainting. Then exhaling is done slowly. This is *mūrcha kumbhaka. Plavini* demands skill on the part of the *sādhaka.* In this the *sādhaka* inhales the air as one drinks water till the stomach is bloated. Later *kumbhaka* should be performed. After this exhalation should be done gradually like belching.

In *Sūryabheda Prānāyāma* inhaling, retention and exhalation are done alternately with the two nostrils. First by closing the left nostril, inhaling should be done through the right nostril, then by closing the two nostrils *kumbhaka* should be performed by using *Jalandhara bandha* technique. Then by closing the right nostril, the air should be released through the left nostril. A similar process should be done with the left nostril. This completes one round and the *sādhaka* must do minimum ten rounds. This *Prānāyāma* also is known as *Nādi Sodha Prānāyāma*. It is an effective *Prānāyāma* in which both body and mind are purified. It destroys the intestinal worms and diseases arising from excess of wind (*vāyu*). It also cures rhinitis, cephalalgia and various sorts of neuralgia.

Ujjayi Prānāyāma is done in the following way: Inhale slowly through both the nostrils in a uniform way till the breath fills the space from the throat to the heart. Retain the breath and then exhale slowly through the left nostril by closing the right nostril. It removes the heat in the head, all the evils arising in the body, increases gastric fire and cures dropsy of the belly, asthma and all sorts of pulmonary diseases. It destroys decay and the *sādhaka* is never affected by the diseases of phlegm, nerves, dyspepsia, dysentery, enlarged spleen, consumption, cough or fever.

In *Sitakari Prānāyāma* first the tongue is folded so that the tip of the tongue touches the upper palate and later the inhaling is done through the mouth with a hissing sound. After this retention should be performed and the air should be released through both the nostrils. It removes hunger, thirst, indolence and sleep. It makes the body acquire vigour, strength and beauty.

Sitali is practised by protruding the tongue a little away from the lips and folding it like a tube. The inhaling is done by drawing the air through the mouth with the hissing sound. After performing the *kumbhaka* with comfort by applying *Jalandhara bandha*, exhaling should be done slowly through both nostrils. This *Prānāyāma* purifies the blood, quenches thirst and appeases hunger. It cools the system and destroys chronic diseases like dyspepsia and inflammation caused by fever, consumption, indigestion, bilious disorders, phlegm, etc. It is said he who practises this regularly will not be affected by the bite of snakes and scorpions. This *Prānāyāma* may be practised in summer while *Bhastrika* in winter which will cure asthma and consumption.

(ii) Kevala Kumbhaka Prānāyāma

All the eight forms of *Prānāyāma* discussed above are related to *Sahita Kumbhaka*, which means *Kumbhaka* is achieved with effort and is coupled with inhalation and exhalation. In another kind, *Kumbhaka* is achieved without effort, and it is known as *Kevala Kumbhaka*. It is not conditioned by time and place; it happens naturally devoid of any effort. In *Vasishta Samhita* it is described as absolute *Kumbhaka*. In this type, the breath ceases suddenly and *Kumbhaka* takes place naturally with ease. The *sādhaka* can retain it as long as he can. But, it must be noted here that this *Kevala Kumbhaka Prānāyāma* cannot be obtained easily by ordinary *sādhakas* for whom the practice of *Sahita Kumbhaka* is a must. It is only by a continuous practice that the *sādhaka* can get *Kevala Kumbhaka Prānāyāma* at the end. For the born sages and advanced yogis, it is easily obtained. Patanjali describes this type as the fourth and the highest kind of *Prānāyāma* in *Sūtra* 51 in the *Sādhana Pāda* (*Bāhyābhyantara-visayāksepi caturthah*).[4] That *Prānāyāma* which goes beyond the sphere of internal and external is the fourth type. This is the real *Prānāyāma*, according to Patanjali. All the previous practices in *Sahita Kumbhaka Prānāyāma* are merely a preparation. With the increased practice of this natural *Kumbhaka Prānāyāma* as described in the *Sūtra* the *sādhaka* attains immense supernatural powers which are detrimental if they are viewed as the ultimate or misused for selfish ends. In *Vasishta Samhita* it is described as the gateway to the rise of *Kundalini*. Natural *kumbhaka* awakens *Kundalini Shakti*, steadies the mind, invigorates the body and increases the longevity. As *kundalini* arises completely the *sādhaka* attains *Nirvikalpa samādhi* in which he tastes the elixir of the triple absolute qualities *sat-chit-ānanda* of *Brahman*, the ultimate reality as described in the *upanishads*. Thus *Prānāyāma* as taught and practised in certain schools has a limited scope. It is viewed as the best technique that invigorates one's health. It is performed as mere routine breathing exercise. This is not *Prānāyāma* as described in the *Vasishta Samhita*, in the *Yoga Sūtras*, in the *Sivayōga Dīpikā* by Sri Sankaracharya.

---

[4]बाह्याभ्यन्तरविषयाक्षेपी चतुर्थः । *Sādhana Pāda, Sūtra* 51.

The *Sivayōga Dīpikā* describes three kinds of *Prānāyāma*: *Prakrita*, *Vaikrita* and *Kevala Kumbhaka*. If the *prāna* is in the form of inhaling and exhaling in a natural way without *Kumbhaka* it is called as *Prakrita*. If it is restrained by *Kumbhaka* according to certain procedures prescribed in the scriptures, it is known as *Vaikrita* or artificial. If *Prakrita Prānāyāma* belongs to mantra yoga, *Vaikrita Prānāyāma* to laya yoga, if *kumbhaka* is achieved naturally, it is called as *kevala kumbhaka*. In the *Yoga Vasishta* (VI:125-76), both the external (*bāhya*) and the internal (*antargata*) *kumbhakas* and their various advantages are described. In *Aparōkshānubhuti* (118-120) Sri Sankaracharya writes that *Prānāyāma* is not mere inhaling and pressing the nose. It is the control of all life-forces and by releasing nothing it is understood that Brahman is in all things, the outgoing breath represents the negation of the universe, the inhaling "I am Brahman", the *Kumbhaka* the permanence of that thought. This is real *Prānāyāma*, according to Sankara and all other forms are for the unknowing.

Benefits of Prānāyāma

The benefits of *Prānāyāma* are varied. Patanjali discusses two results in *Sūtras* 52 and 53. The first benefit is the dissolution of the covering light (*Tatah ksīyate prakāsā varanam*).[5] Many have interpreted it in a wrong way. Actually, the covering of light referred to in this *Sūtra* is not the light of the soul but the light or luminosity associated with the subtler

---

[5]ततः क्षीयते प्रकाशावरणम्। *Sādhana Pāda, Sūtra* 52.

vehicles located in the physical body. Generally, the *Sādhaka* is ignorant of these subtler vehicles located in the dense physical vehicle. Through the practice of *Prānāyāma* the *Sādhaka* realizes the necessary changes in the distribution of *Prāna* in the subtle psychic centres, thereby the physical brain will be able to come into contact with the luminosity more and more. Thus the grossness of subtler bodies is removed and their luminosity is more glaringly revealed to the *Sādhaka.*

The second result of *Prānāyāma* practice is described in *Sūtra* 53 (*Dhāranāsu ca yogyatā manasah*)[6] as it prepares the mind for the practice of *Dhārana, Dhyāna* and *Samādhi—Astānga Yoga.* Through *Prānāyāma* mind becomes like a clarified butter. It acquires the capacity to view and perceive mental images without confusion. This clarity is essential as it facilitates concentration to a great extent. That is why Patanjali has made it an integral part of *Astānga Yoga.*

Besides these two fundamental results accrued in the practice of *Prānāyāma,* it also results in obtaining various *siddhis* such as foretelling, thought reading, levitation, psychometry, clairaudience, moving about unseen, entering the body of another man, the power to remain always young, the power of making the body small or very large, and finally the oneness with *Paramātmā.* The continuous practice of *Prānāyāma* destroys all *Karmas* and the *Sādhaka* gets purified more and more, thereby he becomes subtler and subtler. His body shines, it becomes light, lean

---

[6]धारणासु च योग्यता मनसः। *Sādhana Pāda, Sūtra* 53.

and strong. His voice becomes sweet and his eyes sparkle like pearls. He acquires steadiness in mind and an insatiable thirst for the higher spiritual knowledge.

Prāṇāyāma-regulated Nourishment

Gheranda says that he who begins *Prāṇāyāma* without a regulated diet reaps various diseases and falls short of success. The diet should be carefully regulated and it should be pure (*Sāttvic*). The *Sādhaka* should be strictly vegetarian. He should take such food, *sāttvic* in nature, which gladdens his heart, purifies his body and quietens his mind. Such *sāttvic* food consists of fresh vegetables, fruit, leaves, rice, wheat and millets. He should abstain from bitter, acid, sour, salty and roasted things, curd, alcohol, over-ripe fruit and spoiled vegetables. He should fill half the stomach with food, one quarter with water and the remainder should be kept empty to allow the wind move freely. The *Sādhaka* can eat such food which is easily digestible, enjoyable, tender foods, appropriate to the nourishment of the body. He should abstain from not easily digestible, bad or putrid, very hot or very cold as well as stale food. The diet on the whole ought to be pure, wholesome, nourishing and pleasant. Otherwise, harmony and free flow of the *pranic* currents through the *nādis* do not occur. Likewise, he should abstain from anything injurious to the body or prolonged fasting. Ultimately, common sense should be the hallmark of every true *Sādhaka* or yogi-practitioner. *Prāṇāyāma* should be carried out in a private place, in safety, with plentiful supply of water and pure and fresh air amidst pleasant sorroundings.

Conclusion

Having discussed *Prānāyāma* at length, we come to the question once again: what is *Prānāyāma*? It is not the control of the breath. It is better to consider the word in the combination of *Prāna* and *Āyāma*, where the latter means to extend, to expand, to lengthen—both in time and space. What is it, then, that should be expanded or lengthened? The interval, the gap between inhaling and exhaling. It is a moving from the gross to the very subtle. It implies a going beyond the boundaries of breathing where the *Sādhaka* becomes totally unconscious of the process. In the most subtle way it is embracing the *Paramatma*, attaining the perfect union. True *Prānāyāma* enables the *Sādhaka* to attain supreme harmony and perfect equilibrium of the pranic systems. The purpose of *Prānāyāma* is to achieve harmony and rhythm not only into the systems of irregular and imperfect breathing but also in living. If this is irregular, how can one achieve steady mind which is essential for *Dhārana*, *Dhyāna* and *Samādhi*? In the sudden cessation of breath, an intense, clear, deepening awareness of life is found. In that state of pause the *Sādhaka* experiences peace; the mind then becomes very silent; and when it is further deepened the mysteries of life are revealed. *Prānāyāma*, when properly understood and practised, gradually leads to Raja-yoga and Liberation.

9
PANCHA VRITTĪS

One of the most well known *Sūtras* of Patanjali's *Yoga Sūtras* is "*Yogas citta-vrittī-nirodhah*".[1] It means cessation of *Vrittīs* (modifications) of the mind is yoga. At higher level *citta* is Consciousness, one of the three aspects of *Paramatma* called *Sat-Chit-Ānanda* in *Vedānta*. It is the basis of creation. At the individual level *citta* more or less corresponds to 'mind' of modern psychology but it is much more comprehensive and has the larger field of functioning. In modern psychology 'mind' is confined to the expression of only thought, feeling, emotion and volition. In yogic psychology it is like an intangible screen which enables the light of consciousness to be projected in the manifested world. Its real nature is known only on attaining Enlightenment. *Vrittīs* means "modifications" or "functions". We must understand here, although there is relationship between *citta* and *Vrittīs*, *citta* is not material and therefore, it can never be affected by *Vrittīs* nor can be modififed by *Vrittīs*. It is pure

[1]योगश्चित्तवृत्तिनिरोधः । *Samādhi Pāda, Sūtra* 2.

Consciousness. To realize it, *Vrittīs* created by us, which act as obstacles, have to be eliminated. What are these *Vrittīs*? Patanjali gives us a fivefold classification. They are *Pramāna, Viparyāya, Vikalpa, Nidra* and *Smriti.* This fivefold classification may appear to be odd, but it is perfectly scientific. Let us examine them one by one.

Pramāna (right knowledge) and *Viparyāya* (wrong knowledge) comprise those images that are formed by contact with the external world. *Vikalpa* (fancy) and *Smriti* (memory) comprise those images that are formed without any kind of contact with the objective world. In other words, the images produced are purely internal. They are formed within the mind, independent of the contact with the phenomenal world. They are the images caused by the perceptions of the lower mind.

Pramāna may be translated as right knowledge that is derived from the contact with the objective world. Patanjali identifies three sources in *Sūtra* 7 of *Samādhi Pāda*: *Pratyaksānumānagamah Pramānāni.*[2] It means the facts of right knowledge are based on direct cognition, inference and testimony. The first source of knowledge is *Pratyaksa* (direct) contact with the object. Seeing and experiencing through sense organs is *pratyaksa.* Mere perceiving is involved here. There is another kind of knowledge derived from the source of inference (*anumāna*). It is analytical in nature, intellect is involved here. We employ logic and reasoning. The third source of knowledge is based on testimony (*pramānāni*). Here the past

---

[2]प्रत्यक्षानुमानगमः प्रमाणानि। *Samādhi Pāda, Sūtra* 7.

knowledge is involved. The present fact is cross-checked with the past knowledge. Or we may keep the past knowledge and derive conclusive facts. In all these three cases the images formed correspond to the facts.

Viparyāya is the wrong knowledge. It is based on some kind of contact with the object but the mental images do not correspond with the object. It is of three types: image formed in illusion, delusion and hallucination. In illusion, the object is not perceived as it is but mistaken for something else. Sankara's example, mistaking the rope in the darkness for a snake, may be cited here. Or a mirage on the road or in a desert may be mistaken for a water pool. In delusion false opinion or belief of an object or a person is created. In hallucination one imagines one is seeing or hearing something when no such thing is present. It is the opposite of illusion. All this knowledge is erroneous. But such knowledge derived from illusion, delusion and hallucination is called *Viparyāya.* In *Viparyāya* we are not concerned with the actual object, but only with the images formed of it.

Vikalpa is fancy. Patanjali defines it as *Sabda-jnānānupāti-vastu-sūnyo vikalpah* (*Samādhi Pāda,* Sūtra 9).[3] An image conjured up by words without any substance behind it is *vikalpa.* It is not based on actual experience of the object but it is a pure creation of the mind. It is subjective in nature. Memory, imagination, fancy should be distinguished here. Memory is based upon a previous experience, whereas fancy is a fantastic creation of the mind.

---

[3]शब्दज्ञानानुपाति वस्तुशुन्यो विकल्पः । *Samādhi Pāda, Sūtra* 9.

One is objective and the other is subjective in its nature. Modification may also be caused by such images created in imagination or fancy.

The next modification is caused by *Nidra. Nidra* is of two types—dream sleep and deep sleep. Dream sleep is linked with the waking state. Dream sleep is the other side of the waking state. In the waking state actual experiences with the objects are made. When these experiences are duly recognized and recorded, they are stored in memory and subconscious state. During sleep the subconscious state becomes active, and hence, the past and remote experiences in distorted forms appear in the form of sweet and nightmarish dreams. Such dreams become *pratyāya* (content) of the consciousness and cause modifications. Sometimes these dreams are remembered in the wakeful state. In deep sleep there is no *pratyāya* in the field of consciousness. Even then, according to Patanjali, it causes *Vrittīs.* What actually happens in deep sleep is that as there is no *pratyāya* it creates a blank or a void state. This might be mistaken for *samādhi* state. But actually the mental activity does not stop at all, only the brain is disconnected from the mind and so does not record the activities which are going on in the mind. When the person wakes up, the contact is established again, the brain again becomes the seat of mental activity as before.

The last *Vrittī* is *smriti,* that is memory. Patanjali considers memory as a type of *Vrittī.* Memory is the retention of past experiences in the mind. But these stored up experiences are mere impressions (*samskāras*). When these impressions become active, they cause *Vrittīs* in the consciousness.

After classifying and examining the *Pancha Vrittīs*, let us now consider their *nirōdha*. Patanjali offers us two ways, *abhyāsa* (practice) and *vairāgya* (non-attachment), by which suppression of modifications (*Vrittīs*) can take place. What is *abhyāsa*? *Abhyāsa* includes the practice of *Astānga yoga*, i.e., Yoga with eight limbs, as prescribed by Patanjali. There are other systems and schools scattered in all parts of the world which lay down the conditions of practice for attaining the transcendent state in which all *citta-vrittīs* can be suppressed or eliminated. Each system or school is unique in its own way. The practitioner can adopt any one of these systems that suits his/her temperament. But Patanjali's *Astānga yoga* is unique in several ways as compared to the other systems or schools. It is an experimental science, more comprehensive, holistic, humanistic and spiritual. Its catholicity and authenticity has remained unquestioned even after two thousand years.

Abhyāsa is a simple word, but it requires a tremendous effort of the human will. If the *sādhaka* wants to attain the transcendent state, Patanjali lays down three conditions which must be fulfilled. These conditions are defined in the following *Sūtra*: *Sa tu dīrgha-kāla-nairantarya-satkārāsevitodṛḍha-bhūmih* (*Samādhi Pāda, Sūtra* 14).[4] They are: (i) the practices must be continued for a long time (*dīrgha kāla*); (ii) there should be no interruption (*nairantarya*) and

---

[4]स तु दीर्धकालनैरन्तर्यसत्कारासेवितो दृढभूमि। *Samādhi Pāda, Sūtra* 14.

(iii) the practice should be done with devotion and in a spirit of reverence (*satkāra*).

The perpetuation of practice for a long time without interruption and with devotion and reverence is a must for the *sādhaka* if a fundamental change in nature is to be brought out. The path of yoga appears very fascinating and glamorous in the beginning and many take to it with a view to bring about fruit within a very short time. As this does not happen, they abandon it and get into the world and its pursuits. The path requires spiritual maturity, will power and sacrifice on the part of the *sādhaka*. Generally, in the case of vast majority of practitioners, these are found lacking. Hence, the purpose is defeated, and they find it difficult. Nothing is difficult and impossible for a man if he has the strong sense of will power and perseverance. The *samskāras* we have acquired are so strong and deeply rooted in us that they may create obstacles on the path. Hence, to break them is a strenuous task. No one can predict when the final goal will be attained and therefore, he who treads this path must make up his mind to continue not only for a long time but with devotion and reverence until the goal is reached. When the three conditions mentioned in the *Sūtra* are strictly followed progress on the path of yoga is assured. It may be slow in the beginning but perseverance will firmly establish the *sādhaka* on the path and the attainment of the final goal becomes only a question of time.

The second means by which the suppression of *citta-vrittīs* can be brought is *vairāgya* which means non-attachment. Non-attachment from what? The *vairāgya* contains *rāga* which is defined as the attraction which arises due to pleasure derived from any object or person. *Vairāgya*, therefore, means the absence of any attraction towards objects or persons which give pleasure. Though the word *vairāgya* contains only *rāga,* it implies both *rāga* and *dvēsa* because these two are the opposites and two sides of the same coin, and where there is *rāga* there is bound to be *dvēsa.* So, non-attachment means freedom from both attraction (*rāga*) and repulsion (*dvēsa*) which underlie the meaning of *vairāgya.*

The reason why *vairāgya* plays such an important role in elimination of *citta-vrittīs* is that desire is rooted in both *rāga* and *dvēsa.* Desire is the driving force behind *vrittīs.* It constantly keeps the mind in a state of agitation. Many of us do not realize its influence upon the consciousness. Trying to calm the mind without understanding and eliminating desire is like trying to stop the movement of a boat on the surface of water rocked by a violent strong wind. So if the driving force of desire is not eliminated completely the mind will never come to rest (*niruddha* state). The practice of *vairāgya* is directed towards the object. But *vairāgya* alone is not sufficient. Both *abhyāsa* and *vairāgya* should be jointly utilized for *citta-vrittī-nirōdha.*

In the practice of *vairāgya* we must note that both temporary indifference towards objects and deliberate destruction of desire should be desisted. Deliberate destruction of desire is a violent approach. It leads to neurosis. Also, it should be recognised that isolation from the world or running away from temptations will not help us in acquiring true *vairāgya.* We have to learn to understand the very mechanism of how a desire arises, how it persists and so on. An intelligent way of understanding the operation of desire in the mind will help us realize freedom from the desire itself. This intelligent understanding of desire by using discriminative power is what is known as *viveka.* Real *vairāgya* is not characterised by a violent struggle with our desires. It should come naturally and in its most effective form by the exercise of our discriminative power which is called *viveka.* So, the real weapon in *vairāgya* is *viveka* which is expressed in *Buddhi.* Along with *Vairāgya* and *Viveka, Vichāra* should also be considered. *Vichāra* means inquiry which should be directed towards the higher realms and aspects of life. *Vairāgya, Viveka* and *Vichāra* (called as three Vs) are the three greatest weapons in spiritual life. They may be considered as three aspects of the same process of dissipation of illusion of *vrittīs.* As the process reaches a deeper level, *Jnānōdaya* takes place, that is Enlightenment.

10
PANCHA KLĒSAS

Klēsa means pain or affliction or misery. But gradually it came to acquire the meaning of what causes pain, affliction or misery. We all experience pain or misery in our daily life but we never inquire deeply into its nature because of our deep fascination for life. Buddhistic philosophy identifies desire as the root cause of misery in life whereas Patanjali distinguishes and classifies it as five kinds, *avidyā, asmitā, rāga, dvēsa* and *abhinivesa.* According to him the philosophy of *Klēsas* is really the foundation of the system of yoga.

All the five *klēsas* have their mutual relationships. They are not distinct by each other. They may be likened to a tree. *Avidyā* is the root, *asmitā* the trunk, *rāga* and *dvēsa* are the branches and leaves and *abhinivesa* is the fruit of a tree. These *klēsas* may be found in four states in a human being: in a latent form (*prasupta*), or in a very feeble or tenuous condition (*tanu*) or scattered (*vichchinna*) or in a fully expanded condition (*udāranamu*). It is only in the case of the advanced yogis that the *klēsas* are present in the dormant state. In the case of ordinary people, they are present in the other three conditions, depending upon external conditions, and circumstances.

Avidyā is the first *klēsa.* It means ignorance or lack of awareness of Reality. It is the root cause of the other four *klēsas* which in their turn produce all the miseries of human life. But the word *avidyā* cannot be used in ordinary sense of ignorance or lack of knowledge, but in its highest philosophical sense. It is not the knowledge which we acquire through the intellect. Such knowledge is purely phenomenal in nature. It is bound by time and space. It is subject to change. It is impermanent. A man may be a great scholar, a genius, a walking encyclopaedia. He may mistake all that he sees, learns and acquires for real. Yet he is not aware that he is caught in the great illusions. The real knowledge is that which is unchangeable. It is the knowledge of the Ultimate Reality. This knowledge is not something outside of us. It is all-pervasive. It is *Chit,* the Pure Consciousness, one of the three-dimensional attributes, the other two being *Sat* and *Ānanda.* It is by knowing our true nature the three dimensional quality of the Ultimate Reality will be known. The absence of this knowledge is what is known as *avidyā.* It results in our inability to distinguish between the eternal, pure, blissful Ultimate Reality and the non-eternal, impure and painful not-self. Our progressive involvement in our own matter, phenomenal knowledge deprives us of this Self-knowledge. Hence, we are caught in *avidyā.* Till we realize this state, *avidyā* continues to exist at the individual level.

The second *klēsa* is *asmitā* which is likened with the trunk of a tree. *Asmitā* means 'I am ness'. Patanjali defines it as the identification of the power of consciousness with the power of cognition (*Dṛg-darśana-śaktyor-ekātmatevāsmitā, Sādhana Pāda*: *Sūtra* 6).[1] This is an important idea which we should understand thoroughly. The word *asmita* is derived from '*asmi*' which means literally 'I am'. Here, 'I am' means 'I exist'. What is that which exists for ever. It is the Pure Consciousness. It is eternal. When this Pure Consciousness gets involved in matter and owing to the power of Maya, knowledge of its Real nature is lost. The pure 'I am' changes into 'I am this' and 'I am that'. 'This' or 'that' may be the subtlest vehicle or the grossest vehicle through which the Pure Consciousness works. The two processes, namely, the loss of awareness of the real nature of Pure Consciousness and its identification with its vehicles are simultaneous. The moment Pure Consciousness identifies itself with its vehicles it has fallen from its pure state and it becomes bound by the limitations of *avidyā,* and from it results *asmitā.* More identification with the matter thickens *asmitā.* On the other hand, when the reverse takes place, that is, when the consciousness is released from the matter, the veil of *avidyā* is removed, consequently *asmitā* becomes weaker and subtler.

The identification with a vehicle is not a simple but a very complex process and has many aspects. The vehicle may be a thought, or a piece of emotion, or body, or it may include other accessories and

---

[1]दृग्दर्शनशक्त्योरेकात्मतेवास्मिता। *Sādhana Pāda, Sūtra* 6.

objects in the environment. The greater the identification or association with the vehicle, the thicker the *asmitā* will be. Of all the vehicles *asmitā* manifesting through the physical body is the grossest form of the *klēsa.*

The third *klēsa* is *rāga.* Patanjali defines it as the attraction which accompanies pleasure (*Sukhānusāyi rāgah, Sādhana Pāda, Sūtra* 7).[2] Attraction is due to some kind of pleasure, physical, emotional or mental. We may be addicted to some kind of food because we derive pleasure from it. We may be attached to a person because we desire from him/her some kind of pleasure, physical or emotional. We may be devoted to a particular idea because we derive some intellectual satisfaction from it. Pain is the absence of this pleasure. It arises because we may lose the object or person or idea.

Dvēsa is the fourth *klēsa* which means repulsion. Patanjali defines it as *Dukhānusāyi dvēsah* (*Sādhana Pāda, Sūtra* 8),[3] which means that repulsion which accompanies pain is *dvēsa.* It is the opposite of *rāga.* It is the natural repulsion felt towards any person or object or idea which is a source of pain. *Dvēsa* is only *rāga* in the negative. They together form a pair of opposites. They are like two sides of the same coin. Therefore, transcending one without transcending the other is meaningless. They bind us down to the lower levels of consciousness. The repulsions bind us as much as the attractions. In their gross form they are responsible for much of

---

[2]सुखानुशायी रागः । *Sādhana Pāda, Sūtra* 7.

[3]दुःखानुशायी द्वेषः । *Sādhana Pāda, Sūtra* 8.

human misery and suffering. In the light of this observation, it may be seen that *Vairāgya* is not only freedom from *rāga* but also freedom from *dvēsa.*

The last *klēsa* is *abhinivesa* which means a strong desire for life. Patanjali has defined it as *Svarasvāhī Vidusopitathā rūdho'bhinivesah* (*Sādhana Pāda: Sūtra* 9).[4] When translated it reads like *Abhinivesa* is the strong desire for life which dominates even the learned. It is the fruit of a tree. There are two points in this *Sūtra* which require some explanation. First, it is a fact that every human being wants to cling to life. This strong attachment to life which is universal is well established even in the learned. The learned is as much attached to life as the ordinary person. Second, the *Sūtra* has an important phrase *Svarasvāhī* which means sustained by its own inherent force or potency. The desire to live is not an accidental development in the course of evolution. It is some constant and universal force, very much inherent in life which automatically finds expression in this 'desire to live'. According to the yogic philosophy this force is rooted in the very origin of things and it comes into play the moment consciousness comes in contact with matter and the evolutionary cycle begins. As we have already seen *avidyā* is the root of all *klēsas* and *abhinivesa* is merely fruit or the final expression of the chain of causes and effects set in motion with the birth of *avidyā* and the involution of consciousness in matter.

Further, it may be noted that the different *klēsas* are not unconnected with one another. They form

---

[4]स्वरस्वाही विदुषोअपि तथा रूढ़ोअभिनिवेश: I *Sādhana Pāda, Sūtra* 9.

a sort of series beginning with *avidyā* and ending with *abhinivesa. Abhinivesa* is merely the final phase in the development of the *klēsas* and that is when it is *Svarasvāhī.* Until and unless the tree of *klēsas* is destroyed, root and branch, the pain continues to appear in an unending flow. We will have a series of births. This can be done by a systematic course of yogic discipline as taught by Patanjali. Only by treading the path of *astānga yoga* freedom from the *klēsas* can be brought. Mere knowledge of the intellect is in itself inadequate for freeing a man from the *klēsas.*

The one means by which the *klēsas* can be destroyed is *Dhyāna,* the seventh limb in *astānga yoga* (*Dhyāna-heyās-tad-vṛttayah, Sādhana Pāda, Sūtra* 11).[5] The word *Dhyāna* literally means meditation, but it is a rather comprehensive self-discipline of which meditation is the pivot. In fact, the *klēsas* must be attacked from many sides at once, not merely from one side. Here, the whole technique of *kriya-yoga* will have to be utilized along with *Dhyāna. Svādhyāya, Tapas* and *Īshvara-Pranidhāna* constitute *Kriya-yoga.* But the essential part of all these three is really *Dhyāna,* the intensive meditation in order to understand the deeper problems of life and to solve them effectively for the realization of one's main objective. *Svādhyāya* is a self-study, *Tapas* is purification and *Īshvara-Pranidhāna* is a surrender to *Īshvara.* No success in Yoga is possible unless all the energies of the soul are polarized and harnessed for achieving the central purpose. So the word *Dhyāna*

[5]ध्यानहेयास्तदवृत्तयः। *Sādhana Pāda, Sūtra* 11.

includes *Tapas, Īshvara-Pranidhāna, Sravānam* (hearing), *Mananam* (brooding over the deeper problems of life) and *Nidhidhyāsa,* that is changing habits of thought and attitudes by means of meditation. So the word *Dhyāna* implies all mental processes and exercises which may help the *sādhaka* to reduce the active influence of *klēsas* to the passive condition. It is necessary to note here that reducing the *klēsas* to latent or passive condition does not mean merely bringing them to a temporary state of quiescence. It means making the tendencies so feeble that they are not easily aroused on the one hand, and slowly and gradually, on the other, we must work towards their total elimination. Another point which needs attention is that suppression of one *klēsa* is not adequate, it will assume other forms. Therefore, all the *klēsas* have to be attacked and tackled from all sides. Then the real purpose of yoga is served. This determines the success of the endeavour on the part of the *sādhaka.*

11

NAVA VIKSEPAS

Dhyāna in Patanjali's *Astānga yoga* is the seventh limb which precedes *samādhi*. *Dhyāna* is meditation which is inward-turned (*Pratyak cētana*) as opposed to outward-turned (*Paranga cētana*). An ordinary individual's mind is always outward-turned. It is immersed in the outer world and constantly affected by a series of images that pass. The whole aim of *Dhyāna* is withdrawing the consciousness from without to within, for the ultimate mystery of life is hidden in the very heart or centre of our being and can be found only there and nowhere. The turning-outward of consciousness is caused by *viksepa*. In *Sūtra* 30 in *Samādhi Pāda* Patanjali identifies nine kinds of *viksepas*. They are *Vyādhi* (disease), *Pramāda* (carelessness), *Styāna* (languor, dullness), *Samsaya* (doubt), *Ālasya* (laziness), *Avirati* (hankering after objects), *Bhrānti darsana* (delusion), *Ālabdhabhūmikatva* (non-achievement of a stage, inability to find a footing) and *Anavasthitatvāni* (unsteadiness, instability).

Vyādhi is a disease. If body is diseased, it becomes feeble, and an individual with diseased body can hardly meditate. Therefore, a perfect health is a necessity for treading the path of yoga. That is why Patanjali has included *āsana* and *Prānāyāma* as the first two limbs in his system of yoga. *Styāna* may be considered languor or dullness. One may have good health but lack nerve power and therefore be disinclined to take up any prolonged *sādhana.* This may undermine all efforts to *sādhana.* This fatigue is purely psychological and not physical. A fatigued mind causes *viksepa* to the *sādhaka.*

Samsaya is doubt. A doubtful mind causes *viksepa.* While doing *sādhana* several questions may crop up in the mind of a *sādhaka* such as: What is the use of *Dhyāna*? What purpose can be achieved in *Dhyāna*? Is there really any Reality to be realized or merely pursuing a mirage? Why is man so much interested in things that are not visible and seen? Are the methods he is using really effective? Has he the capacity to go through all the obstacles and reach the goal? These and other doubts of a similar nature may assail his mind resulting in the losing of spirit and abandoning the *sādhana* in the middle. Such doubts may also cause depression. Therefore, the *sādhaka* must develop an unshakable faith (*Shraddhā*) in the efficacy of yoga, in himself and in the methods that he adopts. A doubt may be irrational and illogical, but faith is transrational. A doubt may be contradicted by logic and reason, but faith cannot be. It is above logic and reasoning. Faith results from direct experience. On the basis of faith the *sādhaka* must start his practice and reach the goal. This alone is not adequate. He must also possess an unending endurance to bear with the obstacles that might crop up in the path.

Pramāda is carelessness. This is another obstacle which discourages the *sādhaka* aspiring for higher spiritual life. Some people are careless by nature. Some get it by being overconfident. Carelessness is a weakness which prevents a man from achieving eminence in any field. It makes him lethargic. In the field of yoga it is not only an obstacle but a great danger. A careless yogic practice can ruin his life by causing immense damage to his psyche. Therefore, a *sādhaka* should conquer the habit of carelessness and learn to pay careful attention not only to important things of life but also to those which are considered unimportant.

Ālasya is considered laziness which results in a distracted condition of the mind. It is the result of one's excess indulgence in comforts and luxuries. As one takes to more pleasure yielding actions, one develops laziness. Languor is purely a physical defect while laziness is purely a psychological condition. Both *pramāda* and *ālasya* can be overcome by the regular and uninterrupted practice of *āsana* and *Prānāyāma*. *Avirati* means worldly mindedness. One who is deeply immersed in worldly things will hardly find time to reflect upon the real problems of life. In this world there are thousands and lakhs of people who lead this kind of life without ever pausing and pondering over the problems that confront life. Such people have hardly evolved in mind and spirit. People hankering after world's objects like wealth, honour, name, etc., can never see and recognize the illusions. Wealth may happen or not happen, but these things are temporary. If the *sādhaka* does not see the ephemeral nature in these things, they can be a serious cause of *viksepa*.

Bhrānti darsana means taking a thing for what it is not. It happens due to lack of intelligence and discrimination. It is of two kinds. One is the *sādhaka* may mistake worldly things and objects for real. This happens in all of us. Hence, we hanker after things and objects in the world. Next, a *sādhaka* may begin to experience lights and hear strange sounds of various kinds during his early practices. These experiences are very spurious, and they may be mistaken for having seen God. The *sādhaka* may begin to think that he has made great progress. If the *sādhaka* cannot distinguish between the essential and non-essential things in spiritual unfoldment, his progress is likely to be hampered at every stage. He may tend to get entangled in such spurious experiences which in turn may affect his spiritual *sādhana*. He may not proceed further, and fossilization in spiritual *sādhana* may happen. Hence, the *sādhaka* must resist such temptations, and be extra-cautious and intelligent.

Ālabdhabhūmikatva is an inability to establish oneself in a particular state. As the *sādhaka* continues with his persistent *sādhana* he may pass through different stages, pushing himself into the deeper levels of consciousness. In all these stages, persistent effort is required for the *sādhaka* to put himself firmly in them. If he moves from a lower state to a higher state, he must remain firmly in the latter with persistent effort of the will so that he may not fall back into the former state but on the other it should help him move further deeper. The *sādhaka* with weak heart may not succeed in his efforts. This weakness in heart and the inability to obtain a firm footing can cause distraction and disturb the perfect equanimity of the mind. Therefore, the *sādhaka* must possess inexhaustible patience and capacity for self-surrender in order to overcome this particular weakness.

The last state which causes *viksepa* is *anavasthitatvāni* which means unsteadiness. Both *ālabdha bhūmikatva* and *anavasthi tatvāni* can happen simultaneously in the *sādhaka* if he is mentally weak. The former refers to the inability of the *sādhaka* to establish himself in a particular state, the latter to the reversion to a previous state. Every time when the *sādhaka* advances to a higher state, he may tend to fall back into the previous lower state. In the beginning such mental processes of reversion may happen, the *sādhaka* must not lose his spirit. It is one thing to lose one's foothold in the next stage because of lack of persistent practice and another thing to lose it because of the inherent fickleness of the mind. This causes *viksepa.*

The nine obstacles enumerated by Patanjali are of a particular type. There can be other kinds of obstacles also. *Karma* can place obstacles in the path of the aspirant which may make the *sādhana* impossible for the time being. Similarly, attachment (*rāga*) to objects, persons or ideas and repulsions (*dvēsa*) may frequently hamper the progress. Defects in the character may also stand in the way of the *sādhaka.*

The results of these conditions which cause *viksepa*, Patanjali says, are pain, despair, nervousness and hard breathing (*Dukha-daurmanasyāngamejayatva-svāsa-prasvāsa viksepa-sahabhumvah, Samādhi Pāda, Sūtra* 31).[1] The first of these is pain. Patanjali is not dealing with the fundamental problems of human suffering and misery but with those particular kinds of the mind which produce *viksepa*. Pain is the outcome of inner conflict, torn between the opposite states in the *sādhana*. It may be physical or mental. Physical pain in the yogic *sādhana* is a sign of positive disease while mental pain shows that mind is not in a natural healthy state. The *sādhaka* must examine the latter patiently, of course with great diligence to find its root cause and overcome it and proceed further in his *sādhana*. When the capacity to remove it fails, it leads to despair (*daurmanasya*), it in turn leads to nervousness (*angamejayatva*) and when this reaches a certain degree of intensity, it disturbs the breathing (*svāsa-prasvāsa*) because it disorganizes the flow of pranic currents.

How to overcome these *viksepas*? Patanjali offers us different ways. The first is the constant practice of one truth or principle (*Tat-pratisedhārtham eka-tattvābhyāsah, Samādhi Pāda, Sūtra* 32).[2] Concentration and the capacity to keep the mind directed within are *sin qua non* for the practice of yoga. When these two are developed to a high degree, the *sādhaka* can remove the obstacles that follow naturally. Concentration involves purpose. Purposeless life is

---

[1] दुःखदौर्मनस्याङ्गमेजयत्वस्वासप्रस्वास विक्षेपसहभुंवः । *Samādhi Pāda, Sūtra* 31.

[2] तत्प्रतिषेधार्थमेकतत्त्वाभ्यासः । *Samādhi Pāda, Sūtra* 32.

meaningless. The purpose here being to achieve the higher states of Consciousness to realize the true nature of the Self. The *sādhaka* should acquire the capacity to pursue an objective with energy and perseverance. Then the *viksepas* can be thwarted.

Next, Patanjali, in giving a number of alternative ways for overcoming *viksepas*, defines the correct attitude of a yogi in relation to his environment and other beings. It includes *Maitri* (friendliness), *Karunā* (compassion), *Mudita* (gladness) and *Upēksānam* (indifference)—*Maitri-karunā-muditōpeksānām sukha dukha-punyāpunya-visayānām bhāvanātas citta-prasādanam* (*Samādhi Pāda, Sūtra* 33).[3] One of the greatest sources of disturbances to mind arises from our attitude towards our own environment, our reactions to what people say and their behaviour. We react to the things in a violent way according to our mental make-up. With the result we are constantly disturbed by our own emotional attitudes. Sometimes we do not react but remain indifferent, hard-hearted and calm as if we were not concerned. Both these attitudes are undesirable and cannot lead us to acquire a calm, gentle and compassionate nature in accordance with the requirements of the higher spiritual life. Spiritual life does not accept violent reactions as well as cold and indifferent attitude. It requires a balanced nature in which our reactions should be correctly regulated by the highest motives and are in harmony with Higher Spiritual Laws. To achieve equilibrium, Patanjali prescribes fourfold medicine in the *Sūtra*. The first is *maitri*, that is,

---

[3]मैत्रीकरुणामुदितोपेक्षाणां सुखदुःखपुण्यापुण्यविष याणां भावनातश्चित्त प्रसादनम्। *Samādhi Pāda, Sūtra* 33

developing friendliness towards everyone in which there is no room for enmity. Second is *karunā,* that is, compassion. To be compassionate is to remain one with the whole creation. It is to identify with everything and every creature. In this one attains cosmic oneness. Seeing the life principle in everything but not the forms. Third is *mudita,* that is, remaining glad in all situations, accepting life as it is or as what it offers. Fourth is *upēksānam,* that is, remaining indifferent to happiness (*sukha*), misery (*dukha*), virtue (*punya*) and vice (*apunya*). Though indifference is undesirable in spiritual life, it should be accepted by the *sādhaka* in the beginning. This fourfold conduct is meant for the *sādhaka* who is serious about yogic life and not for the highly enlightened as they have already transcended the limitations. The purpose of this prescription is to refine the mind and remove all *viksepas.* Only then can the *sādhaka* establish himself in *Dhyāna.*

Besides a clarified mind, Patanjali says in another *Sūtra,* a strong and restful nervous system is essential for the practice of yoga. This can be achieved by the practice of *Prānāyāma* (*Pracchardana-vidhāranābhyām vā prānasya, Samādhi Pāda, Sūtra* 34).[4] Through *Prānāyāma* the *nādis,* the channels for the flow of *prāna,* will be purified. If these *nādis* are not purified the currents of *prāna* do not flow in them smoothly resulting in various kinds of nervous disturbances. These manifest chiefly in a general feeling of physical and mental restlessness which cause *viksepa.* If *Prānāyāma* is correctly practised for

[4]प्रच्छर्दनविधारणाभ्यां वा प्राणस्य। *Samādhi Pāda, Sūtra* 34.

a long time, the body becomes light and acquires vitality and the mind attains calm and restful pose.

Another way by which the *viksepas* can be checked is by fixing the mind in some superphysical sensuous cognition (*Visayavati vā pravrttir utpannā manasāh sthiti-nibandhanī, Samādhi Pāda, Sūtra* 35).[5] Such cognition may be brought by concentrating the mind on certain vital centres (*chakras*) in the body. A typical example of this method is *Laya yoga* in which the mind is concentrated on *Nāda* or superphysical sounds which can be heard at certain points within the body. Another example is the practice of *Japa* or a Mantra by which partial contact can be established between the lower and the higher vehicles. These methods may bring about the required condition of steadiness in the *sādhaka*. The *sādhaka*, however, should keep in mind that he should not give undue importance and significance to such methods and begin to imagine that he is making great progress on the path of yoga. Second, he should not allow these experiences to become a mere source of emotional and mental satisfactions. Sometimes, some people may use these methods to escape from stress and strain. If such wrong attitudes are adopted these practices may become hindrances instead of a help in the path of the *sādhaka*.

Also the mind can be fixed on those who are free from attachment (*Vīta-rāga-visayam vā cittam, Samādhi Pāda, Sūtra* 37).[6] Such a mind can check *viksepas*. Those souls who have conquered human

---

[5]विषयवति वा प्रवृत्तिरुत्पन्ना मनसा: स्थितिनिबन्धनी। *Samādhi Pāda, Sūtra* 35.

[6]वीतराग विषयम् वा चित्तम्। *Samādhi Pāda, Sūtra* 37.

passions and risen above *Rāga-dvēsa* are known as *vītarāgas.* They may be great spiritual teachers and Masters. Meditation on such divine incarnations or the enlightened souls will naturally help us acquire freedom from *Rāga-dvēsa* and develop serenity and steadiness of mind. Here, we must note that Patanjali recommends meditation on *vītarāgas* but not on the abstract virtues because the *sādhakas* in the beginning may not derive benefit from such abstract virtues. They may get confused. Whereas on those in whom the virtues are embodied the benefits are easily derived. It is easier to connect oneself with a personality than with an abstract virtue because it brings about a flow of power and influences the *sādhaka* in accelerating the progress.

Finally, Patanjali offers us another method of overcoming *viksepas,* that is, by connecting our thoughts to the knowledge derived from dreams or dreamless sleep (*Svapna-nidrā-jnānālambanam vā, Samādhi Pāda, Sūtra* 38).[7] Patanjali has used two important words, *Svapna* and *Nidra. Svapna* here means sleep with dreams, *Nidra* dreamless sleep (*susupti*). One might ask here what purpose will be served by meditating upon the chaotic dreams that pass through in the *svapna* state? The fact is that *svapna* and *nidra* are not to be understood as mere conditions of the brain during sleep but they are the subtler vehicles into which consciousness passes during sleep. When we go to sleep, the *jīvātmā* leaves the physical body and begins to function in the next subtler vehicle. But the conscious mind functions in

[7] स्वप्ननिद्रा ज्ञानालम्बनम् वा। *Samādhi Pāda, Sūtra* 38.

the subtler vehicle. We can make shuttles between the conscious physical body and the next subtler vehicle with our will power. Psychists can perform this natural miracle.

Nidra is a state of dreamless sleep. It is a still more subtle world lying deeper than the *svapna* state to which a person may slip during sleep. When this happens the physical brain is completely cut off from the activities of the mind and becomes a blank. Though in this state the brain is disconnected the mind works at a higher level and deals with the phenomena of a subtler nature. It is possible to bring down into the physical brain a memory of experiences undergone in these subtler worlds corresponding to the *svapna* and *nidra.* The images drawn from these states are subtler, and if they are not distorted by the physical brain they remain to be pure and authentic. When this can happen out of volition, a person can meditate on such images. As these mental images are subtle, pure, and higher, they can easily wean away the person from the usual images, impressions caused by the objective world. Thus by having an absorbing interest in such knowledge brought into the waking state, the *viksepas* can be checked and the *sādhaka* can have a poised mind with which he can proceed further in his *sādhana.*

12
TWO KINDS OF YOGIS

Patanjali distinguishes two kinds of yogis. The first kind of yogis referred to in Sūtra 19 of *Samādhi Pāda*[1] are called *Bhāva Pratyāya Yogis.* They include *Videhas* and *Prakritilayas. Videha* means bodiless, *Prakritilaya* means 'absorbed in *Prakriti*'. These yogis enter into *samādhi* naturally without undergoing any vigorous self-discipline outlined in *Astānga yoga mārga.* Because of their peculiar physical and mental constitution which they derive from their birth, they possess the capacity to pass into *samādhi* naturally without any effort. Such yogis might have done vigorous *sādhana* in their umpteen previous births. Now, the consolidated efforts made in the previous births are carried over to the present birth, when become ripened they form into a strong *prārabdha karma* from which the capacity to pass into *samādhi* naturally is inherited.

Videhas are the psychists who have a peculiar physical constitution in which the dense physical body can be partially separated from the etheric

---

[1] भावप्रत्यायो विदेह प्रकृतिलयानाम्। *Samādhi Pāda, Sūtra* 19.

double or the *prānamaya kosa.* It is this peculiarity which enables the medium to pass into *samādhi* and exercise some psychic powers. *Prakritịlayas* are those yogis who get absorbed in *prakriti* naturally or otherwise. Sometimes they pretend to have attained *samādhi* but not in real sense. Such a *samādhi* is called *jada samādhi.* Such yogis are pseudo yogis. They may possess powers with which they may try to slip into trance-like state which gives us an impression that they have really attained the state. But, in reality, they haven't. In real *samādhi* the yogi's consciousness becomes merged more and more in the universal consciousness which is *Caitanya.*

The second type of yogis are known as *Upāya Pratyāya Yogis.* They do not acquire *samādhi* naturally by virtue of their birth but they should tread the vigorous path of self-discipline of yoga. Patanjali prescribes four traits which are essential for the attainment of a high spiritual ideal. They are, as mentioned in Sūtra 20 of *Samādhi Pāda, Shraddhā* (faith), *Vīrya* (indomitable energy), *Smriti* (memory), and *Samādhi Prajna* (high intelligence essential for *samādhi*)—*Shraddhā-Vīrya-Smriti samādhi-prajnāpūrvaka itaresām.*[2] Faith is the first trait that a *sādhaka* must possess. It is the firm conviction regarding the presence of the Truth that the *sādhaka* seeks within. It is to be distinguished from belief which is purely mental and sometimes irrational. Whereas faith is related to the whole being. It is transactional. It is unshakable by any rational arguments, whereas belief can be questioned. This faith comes into existence

---

[2]श्रधावीर्यस्मृति समाधि प्रज्ञापूर्वक इतरेषाम्। *Samādhi Pāda, Sūtra* 20.

in our being when our mind is purified and the light of intuition shines. Unless the *sādhaka* has this immense, unshakable, impeccable faith, he can hardly proceed in his *sādhana.* It is an essential requirement for any person to take up spiritual life.

The *Vīrya* is not merely energy, but in itself combines energy, determination, courage, and indomitable will which ultimately overcomes all obstacles and inimical forces that come in the path of yoga. The *sādhaka* should possess this trait which is essential even for an ordinary man to achieve certain things in the material world.

Spiritual life is a long, arduous one. Therefore the *sādhaka* should have the persisting *vīrya* till the goal is realized, which may happen in this life or in several lives. The third trait is *smriti* which is not to be confused with the ordinary psychological sense of memory but it is the experience of the large number of aspirants or the ones who have attained the goal. The *sādhaka* has to acquire the capacity to note the lessons of experience from such enlightened souls and retain them in his consciousness for future guidance. Not only this, the *sādhaka* must have the capacity to learn from his own past experiences. Such learning should prevent the *sādhaka* from repeating the mistakes.

Samādhi prajna is the fourth trait required for the *upāya pratyāya yogis.* It means turning inward constantly and acquiring the high state of intelligence of *samādhi.* It is not to mean the actual state of *samādhi* but knowledge of that state. *Samādhi prajna* precedes *samādhi* which is the real objective of yoga.

Thus we have two kinds of yogis: *Bhāva pratyāya yogis* and *Upāya pratyāya yogis.* If for those *samādhi* happens naturally by birth, they are *Bhāva pratyāya yogis.* If it is attained by following the regular yogic practice, such yogis are known as *Upāya pratyāya yogis.* As we have already seen, in the case of *Bhāva pratyāya yogis,* there might be the cases of pseudo yogis. But in the case of *Upāya pratyāya yogis,* there is no room for pseudo yogis because in their case *samādhi* is attained by virtue of constant practice of yogic discipline. Progress is achieved by earnestness and effort. Until the state is realized the *sādhaka* will not rest. Once he is on the path, it makes him work hard, it rekindles his spirit. As a result his efforts are doubled, trebled and multiplied. As the *sādhaka* deals with his own mind, he can intensify his efforts. When such a person is serious, nothing really stands between him and the goal of *samādhi.* So, what is required for *upāya pratyāya yogis* is the intensity of desire which is a *sine qua non* of rapid progress. There is no limit for sincere aspiration. In fact if the intensity and earnestness of desire is great and persisting, realizing the state of *samādhi* can be instantaneous in this birth itself. If the degree of intensity is feeble, it may take several births. If the desire is intensive, all obstacles will not stand in the way. They just melt away. The *sādhaka* can easily overcome all the initial hurdles and make quick and rapid progress.

13
TWO KINDS OF SAMĀDHI

The Sanskrit word *samādhi* is a combination of two words, *sama* and *ādhi. Sama* means 'balanced' or 'equilibrium', *ādhi* means 'in the beginning'. In the beginning of Creation everything was in a perfect state of balance, harmony and peace. A person who attains this state is a *jnāni.* It also denotes an advanced stage of meditation in which there is a conscious experience of the Higher Reality. This can be attained only by the still mind. That still mind adorned with limitless supreme self alone is *Samādhi.* To put it in other words, when the mind is in communion with the Higher Reality in darkness, it is called *nidra* (sleep). If the immersion is in a conscious and wakeful state it is called *samādhi.*

Patanjali deals with the two varieties of *samādhi* called *Samprajnāta* and *Asamprajnāta.* We have learnt that *samādhi* is an attainment of the Higher Reality, in the still mind. In other words, the Higher Reality can express itself depending upon the particular grade of the mind. If it is coarser, it will have limited expression of that state. *Samādhi* represents this progressive expression in different grades of mind. That is, if the mind becomes higher and lighter released from the clutches of gross matter, the expression of the Higher Reality becomes easier and quick. Patanjali deals with these different grades of the mind as it ascends from the lower and the manifestation of the Higher Reality.

In the two kinds of *samādhi* the common word is *prajnā* which stands for the Higher Consciousness. It is derived from *Pra* which means high, *jnā* which means 'to know'. *Samprajnāta Samādhi* means *Samādhi* with *Prajnā*; *Asamprajnāta Samādhi* means not the *samādhi* with *prajnā*. This is simplistic way of distinguishing. The actual difference lies in the presence or absence of a *pratyāya* in the field of consciousness. *Pratyāya* means the total content of the mind. Here the mind is used in a wider sense and not in the sense of intellect. This *pratyāya* contains images, impressions, principles or the vision of unity of life or it may be of any kind and may exist on any plane of the mind.

In *Samprajnāta Samādhi* Patanjali says *pratyāya* is present in consciousness and the consciousness is directed to it. Whereas in *Asamprajnāta Samādhi* there is no *pratyāya* and therefore there is nothing to draw the consciousness outwards and hold it there. The presence of *pratyāya* in consciousness and the receding from it happens successively in each plane in a progressive manner, until the yogi takes the final plunge from the subtlest plane into Reality itself, that is, the consciousness of the Purusa. In each *Asamprajnāta* state the receding from *pratyāya* creates a blank state which is temporary, which might be mistaken for the consciousness of Reality. So, the yogi should be cautious as not to be trapped in it, he should with perseverance move ahead, cross over each such plane until he reaches the final state of Reality. Whereas his consciousness becomes one with it. How long this process will go on depends on the efforts of the yogi. If the yogi's will power is feeble, he may remain at the lower planes. On the other if his will power is strong, he may attain the state in a short time. Besides, his progress depends on his past *samskāras* which he brings from his previous lives.

Patanjali identifies four stages of unfolding consciousness: *Vitarka, Vichāra, Ānanda,* and *Asmita* respectively. These four stages correspond to the four stages of gunas, namely, *Visesa, Avisesa, Linga* and *Ālinga.* In the first stage of *Samprajnāta Samādhi* the consciousness is centred in the lower mental world and functions through the *Manomaya kosa.* The essential function of the mind in this stage is denoted by the word *Vitarka.* Here the yogi leaves the lower physical body and enters into astral body and functions. Here he may acquire certain clairvoyant powers and bring down the knowledge he has gained into the physical brain when he returns. The *guna* identified in this stage is *Visesa.* It obviously refers to the lower mind which sees all objects as particular things with names and forms and distinguished as having a separate and independent existence and identity. In this stage differentiation of a particular object from others is clearly made and seen.

After practising the first stage the yogi moves

into the next higher plane where consciousness functions through the *Vijnanamaya kosa* or the causal body (*Kārana sarira*). The essential function of the mind working through this vehicle is called *vichāra.* The *guna* identified in this stage is *Avisesa* which means universal or non-specific. Here mind deals with archetypes, universals and principles which underlie the world of names and forms. *Vitarka* isolates a particular object from all the rest whereas *Vichāra* isolates a particular concept, archetype, law or universal principle from all such *Sūksma Visayas.* In this state of *samādhi* the mind is completely isolated from the outer world, and is fused with the object in a state of abstraction which an ordinary man cannot understand.

After passing through the second stage, the yogi enters into another higher stage and functions through *Ānandamaya kosa.* The essential function of the mind working through this vehicle is *Ānanda* and the *guna* identified with this stage is *Linga* in which particular objects and even principles are mere marks or signs which serve to distinguish from other objects. Here in this state of consciousness the intellect is transcended and the supramental consciousness is expressed through *Buddhi,* that is, intuition. In this stage of *Gunas* all objects and universal principles become part of a universal consciousness. Hence, this stage is called *Linga.* Though all these objects and universal principles are embedded as one in consciousness, they are still distinguishable and recognizable. Each object is itself and yet part of a whole. It is a condition of unity in diversity.

The last stage, the fourth stage is called *Asmita*. Here consciousness functions through *Ātman*. The *Guna* identified with this stage is *Ālinga* which is without mark or differentiating characteristic. In this stage the objects and principles lose their separate identity. According to the highest conception of the Vedanta philosophy all objects, archetypes, everything in the manifested universe is modification of consciousness—*Brahma vṛtti*. In the *Linga* stage awareness of objects exists side by side with the awareness of consciousness. In the *Ālinga* stage only awareness of the Divine Consciousness remains. A concrete example to explain these four states is as follows: When pots of different shapes and forms with painted colours are seen as separate objects, one different from the other, this stage corresponds to the *Visesa*. Suppose we see them as pots with a common function of preserving water, this stage is *Avisesa*. If we see all the pots as made of mud, the common substream, as the pot maker sees, this stage corresponds to *Linga*. Lastly, we may see only the mud and not be conscious of the separate pots with a common function, this stage is analogous to the *Ālinga*.

We have seen the four stages in *Samprajnāta Samādhi* which correspond to four *gunas*, each stage succeeding the other and finally reaching the state of pure consciousness devoid of *pratyāya*. All these four stages of *Samprajnāta Samādhi*, it may be noted here, are comprised in *Sabīja Samādhi*. The reason is that the seed (*bīja*) has different kinds of layers, the outermost layer forming the protective and least essential part and the innermost layer or core forming the real or essential part of the whole seed. So, in order that we may get at the core, we have to tear open the different layers one after another until we reach the core. Hence, the *Samprajnāta Samādhi* is called *Sabīja Samādhi* and *Samyama* is performed on some 'object' which is called 'seed'. We can come into touch with the different layers of the object or 'seed' by splitting it open mentally through the technique of *Samādhi.* Each successive stage of *samādhi* reveals to our consciousness a different and deeper layer of the reality of the object and by continuing the process of *Samyama* through the successive stages we ultimately arrive at the innermost reality of the object.

Nirbīja Samādhi (Seedless) can come only when all the four states of *Samprajnāta Samādhi* have been crossed. So, *Sabīja Samādhi* may be called objective *samādhi* whereas *Nirbija Samādhi* as subjective *samādhi* in which there is no 'object' or 'seed' of meditation. What distinguishes *Sabīja Samādhi* from *Nirbīja Samādhi* is the presence of an object associated with *Prakriti* whose relative reality has to be realized. In *Nirbīja Samādhi, Purusa* who is beyond the realm of *Prakriti* is the 'objectless' objective. He is the seeker as well as the object of the search. In *Sabīja Samādhi* he is veiled. In *Nirbīja Samādhi* he attempts to tear off the last veil in order to obtain a completely unobstructed vision of Himself. This is what is meant by Self-Realization.

14
KARMA AND YOGA

Man is bound to the cycle of *Samskāras* (impressions), *Vāsanās* (desires) and *Karmas* (actions). All these enmesh the man in the round of births and deaths. All schools of Indian philosophy accept the Doctrine of Karma and how it conditions human life to the repeated births and deaths. Breaking this cycle is what is referred as *moksa* in Vedantic philosophy and *Nirvāna* in Buddhistic philosophy.

The Doctrine of *Karma* is one of the four essential pillars on which the edifice of Vedantic philosophy stands. The law of *Karma* essentially means that our actions produce results in two ways—in the first place as effects in the shape of happiness and sorrow we reap, and in the next place as actions produce impressions on our minds, the sum total of which forms our character. Our future life is guided by our deeds and our desires in the present life.

Let us first gain more complete picture of how subconscious impressions, desires and *Karmas* operate within the realm of conditioned existence to produce and maintain the vehicle of *Karmas*. The cycle of transmigration in Indian philosophy can be explained in terms of twelve independent factors, which shape the characteristics and problems of everyday existence. These twelve factors are *Avidyā* (nescience), *Samskāras* (subliminal impressions), *Asmita* (I am ness), *Nāma rūpa* (subjective-objective appearances), *Bhāva rūpa* (the transient nature of phenomenal world), *Indriyas* (faculties of actions and perceptions), *Vāsanās* (tendencies), *Upādana* (moving toward an object of desire), *Anubhava* (experience), *Janma* (birth), *Jara* (old age) and *Mrityu* (death).

Avidyā (nescience) is the primal cause which directly or indirectly sets in motion the other eleven factors. *Samskāras* are the encapsulated past *karmas*, triggered by current effects into releasing desires into the streams of consciousness. *Asmita, Nama-rupa, Bhava-rupa* and *Indriyas* are the effects caused by *avidyā* and *samskāras*. *Nāma-rūpa* connotes the subjective-objective world of forms, while *Bhāva-rūpa* reflects the becomingness of the external world, with its cyclical processes of growth and decay. This *Nāma/Bhāva rupa* is directly perceived through the five cognitive senses (*Jnānedriyas*) and indirectly by the *Mānas* (through reason, imagination, etc.). All these combine to create our objective worldview. They also create appropriate subliminal impressions from the subconscious into our conscious mind-stream.

Vāsanās, Upādana and *Anubhava* represent the present causes. *Vāsanās* indicate the motive force given to *samsaric* impulses, which snowball into irresistible compulsions, attractions, etc., which move in the direction of *Upādana* which reflects the thought power to determine how the respective objects of desire can be obtained. *Anubhava* connotes the actual process of attaining and experiencing the objects of desire through the *panchendriyas*. This *anubhava* in turn creates new subconscious impressions (*Samskāras*).

Janma, Jara and *Mrityu* represent the future effects of past as well as present *karmas*. The combined weight of an individual's collective subconscious impressions and the effects of *karmas* that we perform in day-to-day life will take us from *janma* (birth) to *jara* (old age) and finally *mrityu* (death).

What happens during one's existence, the innumerable *karmas* in the form of thoughts, words, and actions form into subliminal impressions that carry forward with the subtle body from one life to the next. This means that the *karmas* of the present life lead to the *karmas* of future lives. They establish a continuous and unending chain of causes and effects. The subconscious impressions (*samskāras*) represent our unripened *karmas*. When these accumulated *karmas* ripen during any given lifetime, we reap good or bad experiences according to the nature of the ripened *karmas*. Until the seeds of *karmas* are broken up, they will go on sprouting into new *karmas* which will consequently leave new subconscious impressions which result in the cyclical repetition of birth and death. But when our *karmas* are completely burned up and done away with all our subliminal impressions, accumulated through an endless series of lifetimes, they are simultaneously nullified. Then the great liberation takes place, that is, the release from the cyclical birth and death.

The law of *karma* is inescapable. It is simply defined as the application of Newton's third law of motion at the metaphysical level. That is, each and every action will yield corresponding good or bad results in terms of happiness and suffering. Every *karma* performed leaves its mark or trace in the form of subliminal impression (*samskāra*) that follows the soul like a shadow into the next life. Thus we perform countless *karmas,* all these will get accumulated which are difficult to be wiped out in a single lifetime. So everyone leaves with his/her many *karmas* that remain unresolved. These unresolved *karmas* become the latent power which motivates us to come back to this Earth to taste the fruits. Thus, life or existence is an unbroken and inexorable process of the fructification of the consequences of our actions performed during earlier phases of existence.

The *karma* philosophy is often mistaken for fatalistic according to which there is no use in struggling against what has already been determined according to which the past *karmas* determine one's future. It is true that the results of *karmas* already committed cannot be annulled or escaped. To that extent our present lives are predetermined. But the results of the past actions alone cannot constitute our life which spreads over years. So, we have years of life to be lived in and we cannot simply remain without performing actions. But, while performing actions, we can be cautious, in the sense that we can use our right of free will and act in a good way or a bad way, shaping the course of our life. This means that we have liberty to shape the destinies of our own life. Thus, we can be the makers of our own destiny by performing either good or bad actions, here and now. In this sense we can be the true architects of our own future and not slaves to fate. So instead of sitting back and passively accepting fate or destiny, we should actively try to improve our lot by performing fresh *karmas* with proper understanding of the law of *karma.*

In the foregoing paragraphs we have discussed the *karmas* as effects and causes. We shall now examine various dimensions of *karma. Karma* includes every conceivable mode of conscious human expression and behaviour. This means that every thought, word and action we perform is recorded in our subconscious and will eventually affect our lives, depending on the motive, intensity, etc. of the *karmas* committed. Another way of classifying *karmas* is in terms of their context in time, according to which *karma* is of three types: *Vartamāna karmas, Prārabdha karmas* and *Sanchita karmas. Vartamāna karmas* include those actions performed in the present will ripen in the future. Here there is full scope to use our own free will and act accordingly using our discrimination for harmonious spiritual advancement and unfoldment. *Prārabdha karmas* are those *karmas* done in the past lives fructifying now. This type of *karma* provides tutelary experience so that we can learn lessons from their effects and improve future performance. As far as these *karmas* are concerned there is no escape from them for everyone. *Sanchita karmas* are unripened actions performed during previous lives. They remain in the subconscious as impressions until they become ripe and begin to fructify in some future life. To these three categories may be added the fourth one, that is, *Āgāmi Karma* which means those actions that are as yet not committed but that will be performed at appropriate time during the course of one's present life.

In reference to actual time of ripening, *Karmas* are classified into *Sopakrama karmas* and *Nirūpakrama karmas.* The former refer to those actions that bear fruit quickly within the lifetime, the latter are those actions that yield their results more slowly, either within this lifetime or in a future incarnation. Another mode of classifying *karmas* is purely by motive. In this mode all *karmas* are divided into two types: *Sakāma Karma* and *Nishkāma Karma.* The former is performed with desire and the latter without desire. It is important to note here that the *Ātman* (Self) does not and cannot by definition perform *karmas.* Only an embodied soul (*Jīva*) performs *karmas,* the effects of which stick to its inner bodies as subliminal impressions (*Samskāras*). These *Sakāma Karmas* are responsible for the cyclical repetition of birth and death. *Nishkāma Karmas* do not bind the *jīva* in any way.

The *Sakāma Karmas* can be further divided into three categories: *Nishiddha Karmas, Kartavya Karmas* and *Kāmya Karmas. Nishiddha Karmas* are those actions which are forbidden in the scriptures of every religion. They include stealing, lying, adultery, cheating, causing injury to others, thinking hateful thoughts, etc. This type of *karmas* are also called

Vikarmas because they retard evolutionary progress. *Kartavya Karmas* are those actions which are prescribed in every religion or in every culture as beneficial or obligatory. They include practising austerities, devotion to God, giving alms to the poor, observing prayer, self-sacrifice, straightforwardness, serving one's parents, discharging one's family obligations, moderation in diet, simplicity, etc. These *karmas* accelerate the evolution of the soul and the elevation of consciousness. They make the *Sattva Guna* in us, which is an essential condition for ascending into higher levels of consciousness. *Kāmya Karmas* are those that are prompted by self-interested motives and desires. They are optional. They are generally performed for the attainment of some particular objects or with a view of future gain. *Karmas* performed to conceive children, obtaining riches or to earn reputation are examples of optional actions.

After analysing the different aspects of *Karmas,* let us now turn to the question, how to break this *karmic* cycle. Breaking this cycle is *moksa* or *nirvāna.* While Samkhya philosophy mainly deals with the involutionary process which binds the individual soul into matter, Yoga philosophy addresses the evolutionary or reverse process by which a soul can obtain release from the fetters of matter and *karmas.* Yoga prescribes the definite psychophysical techniques (*Astānga yoga*) by which the cycle of birth and death is broken. We have learnt that we have no control over the *Prārabdha Karma* and *Sanchita Karma* because both deal with the actions performed in the previous life and the consequences are to be reaped in the present life. But we can exercise control over *Vartamāna Karmas* which deal with the actions to be performed in this life. These can be done by exercising our discretionary, discriminatory power. The five don'ts of *Yama* (*Ahimsā, Satya, Āsteya, Aparigraha* and *Brahmacharya*) and the five dos of *Niyama* (*Saucha, Santosa, Tapas, Svādhyāya* and *Īshvara Pranidhana*) are highly beneficial in performing our right actions. By following these *Yama* and *Niyama* we can perform those actions which are good, thereby the accumulation of unnecessary subliminal impressions (*Samskāras*) in the subconscious state can be checked. As we perform good *karmas* the effects will also be good and the influence of *samskāras* will be less resulting in the positive evolution of soul.

Next, by performing *Nishkāma Karma* forming of subliminal impressions can be totally eliminated. Man cannot remain without performing actions. Only the dead remain so. In the *Bhagavad Gita* Lord Krishna says, "One cannot succeed even for a second in giving up all *karmas.*" Even the advanced yogi cannot escape from them. The question is, therefore, how they should be done. The advanced yogi remains stainlessly unaffected by the consequences. Again in the *Gita*, Lord Krishna says "He who sees action in inaction and inaction in action is a wise man and yogi; he is fully accomplished in karma." This means that a yogi who has attained the knowledge of the self (*Ātma jnāna*) understands the *akarma* in *karma*, that is, inaction in action. Here, the yogi, as he becomes the Self, realizes that he is not the real doer because the ego in him has been completely annihilated. It is the Self that responds to the demands of situations. Just as a yogi sees the inaction in action, the yogi also sees action in inaction. That is, when absorbed in deep meditation, although he may be motionless in one place for hours on end, the soul is capable of moving in any part of the universe, performing innumerable activities. This is known as *karma* in *akarma.* To understand this complex mechanism, one has to first transcend the realm of *karma* itself through the mastery of desireless actions (*Nishkāma Karma*). Such a person is a yogi, perfect in knowledge and untouched by the Law of Karma. Even while occupied with the activities of life, he is ever immersed in the actionless nature of the real self.

15

YOGIC WALKING FOR RELAXATION

Man is basically a walker. Nature has provided him with two legs meant for walking. The primitive man was a great walker. He used his two legs for hunting. Later, as time went by man started using animals like horse, elephant, camel and donkey as means of transport. Technology has, however, replaced these primitive means by cycles, cars, trucks, buses, trains and aeroplanes. As a result, man has stopped using his two legs extensively, but relied more and more on automobiles. Now, man uses two legs for minimal purposes. In this context walking as a form of exercise has gained importance in the fast changing technological world.

Walking is being widely recognized as the best panacea for the lazy and the diseased, and loved by the fun-seekers. It is more popular among the old than among the young. For the old it is the best form of physical exercise because they do not fit in any form of vigorous, strenuous physical exercise. Its increasing popularity is evidently seen in a number of clubs and associations that have come up in big cities and towns to promote it vigorously among all sections of the society.

Walking is more popular among the old in the Western cities and towns. It is a common sight in many Western cities and towns the old and the middle aged taking long walks and strolls along the avenues, bridges, streams, rivers, seas, canals, rail roads and in the parks. In India too, we find similar scenes in major cities and towns.

People suffering from chronic diseases are often advised by the doctors to take brisk walks either in the evening or in the morning in order to tone up their muscles, increase the blood circulation and the intake of more oxygen for purification of blood. But, interestingly and strangely, it is seen more as a form of physical exercise than anything that can really bring in good relaxation to the whole organism. Human system has to be studied and understood in its totality comprising body and mind, and not in parts. Body is not separate from mind, and mind from body. Mind is an integral part of body. As such any exercise that aims at body is not complete. But, unfortunately, all forms of exercises are tuned towards toning up the muscles of body. These are not directed to mind. The reason is, mind is a complex mechanism that needs an altogether different approach to understand.

Walking as practised by the old and the young is unsystematic, unorganised, irregular, unrhythmic and chaotic. Most walkers do a brisk walking as they think and feel it is right. They hardly realize that it brings in more harm to the body than benefit. Such walkers, I see, perspire a lot, and they think at the end that they have done a good exercise. Similarly, while walking, I have noticed, people bend their heads, stoop their body and do not maintain a perfect balance in gravitational pull of the earth. This again does not bring any positive effect on the body, even if one takes a long walk every day. Yet another defect, I have discovered, is that people think more of their problems and miseries while walking. They do not become conscious of the surroundings. Walking, indeed, if done in a proper way, must refreshen your body and mind. But it is not the case as observed. Further, many walkers wear tight garments or coarse T-shirts, and jeans. These garments, it should be noted, affect the skin of the body negatively.

Yogic walking, on the other, introduces several benefits to man. It is called 'yogic' because both mind and body are not treated as separate entities but integrated, thereby a perfect rhythm is created in walking. Not only is harmony created within the system but also with the environment. It brings in a total relaxation to the whole system. It rejuvenates and enthuses the walker. It makes one more active, energetic and confident to cope with the stress and strain of the modern world in an effective way. Yogic walking is a meditative walking. It deals with body and mind effectively. It is much useful to the depressed, diseased and despondent.

Now let us know how it is done. The following are the steps involved in yogic walking:

i) First, before taking walk, wash your body.

Cleansing body is a primary requirement. Later wear loose garments, preferably woven with cotton that can absorb the sweat easily. During winter, a little warm clothes are preferable.

ii) Sit quietly for a few minutes and prepare yourself for a walk mentally and physically. Leave all your thoughts and troubles. When you feel that you are really ready, you can proceed. As you come out from your home, feel the vastness of the sky, you are entering into the infiniteness.

iii) Follow these instructions: keep your head straight, body erect, feet firm to the ground. There should be no tension in the body. It should be free and relaxed. All muscles must be let loose. Do not hold them tightly. If you feel a particular part of the body is contracted and tense, loosen it immediately.

iv) Start walking slowly and leisurely. This slow pace is a must in the beginning. Do not walk fast as if something had to be fulfilled urgently. This sense of urgency should go.

v) As you walk, look round and watch. Watch the sky, clouds, sun, trees, birds, animals, human beings and in fact, everything in nature. Do not be unconscious of your surroundings because you are part of it. Sense and feel every object that you touch. Listen to all sounds that come from all corners. Do not negate them. Watch, listen and feel, but do not think of anything. Do not investigate anything.

vi) Stop and proceed. Take every phenomenon

into account. Watch intently and keenly. Do not have superficial watching. Do not do it mechanically. It should be natural and your response to everything in nature should be spontaneous and unenforced.

vii) Relax and relax. Every piece of observation must bring you solace, comfort, peace and happiness. Embrace nature, love nature and walk. Nature in turn loves you, gives you abundant peace and happiness.

viii) Keep this principle in mind. Do not harm any creature, do not trample it knowingly. This is a violence, and it is against the principle of yogic walking. It is good if you help creatures struggling for life. Be sympathetic and kind.

ix) Walk in this way as far as you can. Do not exceed your capacity. Yogic walking conserves energy and does not waste it. You should not feel tired. If you are tired, the purpose is defeated. Yogic walking does not make you tired: on the other, it rejuvenates you, it provides complete relaxation to your body and mind.

x) In yogic walking you are alone, but you are with the nature. You should not take anyone with you. You should walk alone in utter silence.

xi) Breathing is an important component in yogic walking. It should be rhythmic and not uneven. Take more oxygen naturally and not forcibly. Exhale slowly and steadily. It should be longer than the inhalation.

xii) As you return from walking, lie down in *savāsana* for ten minutes. This should be done correctly, not as you like. The correct posture of this *āsana* is as follows:

Stretch a mat on the flat floor. Remove your garments and wear drawers. Sit with two legs stretched in front with your back erect, and the chin straight. Look straight. Take three or four normal breathings. Then, take a deep breath and as you exhale lower your body slowly until the back touches the floor. Loosen your feet and maintain one foot distance between the two feet. Release your two hands. Bring them a little away from the hips. Loosen every part in the body. Gently close your eyes and watch your breath, until it quietens. Remain in this state for ten minutes. When you feel you are totally relaxed, then turn on the left side. Keep the body straight, right leg resting upon the left leg. Rest your head on the left hand stretched far back. Remain in this state for one to two minutes and slowly as you breath in, get up. As you get up, fold the legs and return to the normal position.

xiii) After *savāsana*, you may walk into the bathroom and take bath. After washing, dab your body with a cotton towel that can quickly absorb the water. Now wear the clothes neatly washed and pressed. Do not wear soiled clothes or clothes which smell badly. You feel you are highly rejuvenated. This is yogic walking.

Practise daily wherever you are, and reap its immense benefits.

16

YOGA AND AYURVEDA

Yoga and Ayurveda are sister sciences. Both have inseparable relationship. Yoga clubbed with Ayurveda will produce positive effect on health. Both belong to the ancient Indian tradition. Both comprehensively illuminate the basic laws and principles governing life on earth. To understand both is to understand the forces that engender our well-being as well as those that lie at the root of existence.

Ayurveda encompasses not only science but religion and philosophy as well. In Ayurveda the whole of life journey is considered to be sacred. Ayurveda is a science of truth as it is expressed in life. All Ayurveda science and literature is based on the Samkhya philosophy of creation. This system was evolved from the Rishis who perceived that there is a close relationship between man and the universe. According to them the source of all existence is cosmic consciousness, which manifests as male and female energy—Shiva and Shakti like Ying and Yang in Chinese philosophy. Rishi Kapila discovered twentyfour principles or elements of the universe, of which *Prakriti* or creativity is the most basic. *Purusha* is the male energy while *Prakriti* is the female energy. *Purusha* is formless, colourless and beyond attributes and takes no active part in the manifestation of the universe. *Prakriti* has form, colour and attributes. It is awareness with choice. It is divine will. *Prakriti* creates all forms in the universe, while *Purusha* is the witness to this creation. It is primordial physical energy containing the three attributes or *gunas*: *sattva* (essence), *rājas* (movement) and *tāmas* (inertia), which are the foundation for all existence.

The Ayurveda is a Sanskrit term meaning 'science of life', '*Ayu*' means 'life' or 'daily living' and '*Veda*' is 'knowing'. It was first recorded in the Vedas. It is considered to be the upaveda of *Atharvaveda* and thus has its origins from the Vedas. It has survived through two sets of original authentic texts each consisting of three books, namely, *Vriddhattrayi*, the three big books: *Charak Samhita* (500 BC), *Sushruta Samhita* (500 BC) and *Samhita of Vāgbhatta* (600 AD); and *Laghuttrayi*, the three small books: *Mādhav Nidāna* (900 AD), *Sārangdhara Samhita* (1300 AD) and *Bhāva Prakāsa* (1600 AD).

All these texts were originally written in Sanskrit and are in the form of an encyclopaedia dealing with all aspects of life, health, disease and treatment. The approach is essentially philosophic, holistic and humanistic. Ayurveda is more life and health oriented than disease and treatment oriented. It presents a total life science and visualizes the total health of an individual in holistic way. It was a well developed system of medicine even in ancient times.

It advocates a complete restorative, preventive and curative system of medicine and appears to have been practised in ancient times in the form of eight major specialities: *Kāya Chikitsā* (general medicine), *Salya Tantra* (surgery), *Salakya Tantra* (disease of eye, ear, nose and throat), *Kaumārabhritya* (paediatrics, obstetrics, and gynaecology), *Rasāyana Tantra* (nutrition, rejuvenation and geriatrics), *Vijikarana* (sexology), *Bhūta Vidyā* (psychiatry) and *Agada Tantra* (toxicology).

This healing system has been practised in India for more than 5000 years. Ayurveda teaches that man is a microcosm, a universe within himself. According to the teachings of Ayurveda every human being has four biological and spiritual instincts: religion, financial, procreative and the instinctive toward freedom. To fulfil these instincts balanced and perfect good health is the foundation. It is a medical metaphysical healing life science.

Ayurveda evolved in the meditative minds of seers of truth, the rishis. They perceived that consciousness was energy manifested into the five basic principles or elements—ether (space), air, fire, water and earth. Man is microcosm of nature and so five basic elements present in all matter also exist within each individual. Ether, air, fire, water and earth, the five basic elements, manifest in the human body as three basic principles or humours known as the *tridosha—vāta, pitta* and *kapha*. These three elements govern all biological, psychological and consciousness levels. They govern the creation, maintenance and destruction of bodily tissue and the elimination of waste products from the body. Thus, the *tridosha* are the foundation of the psychosomatic existence of man.

Throughout life, there is a ceaseless interaction between the internal and external environment. The external environment comprises the cosmic forces (macrocosmic) while the internal forces (microcosm) are governed by the principles of *vāta-pitta-kapha.* Ayurveda holds that a balance should be struck between these two movements. It says that one may create balance in the internal forces working in the individual by altering diet and habits of living to counteract changes in his external environment.

According to Ayurveda, a clear understanding of the *tridosha* should take place for healing oneself. *Vāta* is a principle of movement. It is formed from the two elements ether and air. It governs breathing, blinking of eyelids, movements in the muscles and tissues, pulsations in the heart. It also governs such feelings and emotions as freshness, nervousness, fear, anxiety, pain, tremors and spasms. The large intestine, pelvic cavity, bones, skin, ears and thighs are the seats of *Vāta.* If the body develops an excess of *vāta,* it will accumulate in these areas.

Pitta is translated as fire. It governs digestion, absorption, assimilation, nutrition, metabolism, body temperature, skin colouration, the lustre of the eyes and also intelligence and understanding. Psychologically, *pitta* arouses anger, hate and jealousy. The small intestine, stomach, sweat glands, blood, fat eyes and skin are the seats of *pitta. Pitta* is found and formed from the two elements, fire and water.

Kapha is water. It lubricates the joints, provides moisture to the skin; helps to heal wounds. It gives biological strength, vigour and stability, supports memory retention, provides energy to the heart and lungs and maintains immunity. It is present in the chest, throat, head, sinuses, nose, mouth, stomach, joints, cytoplasm, plasma and liquid secretions of the body such as mucus. Psychologically, *Kapha* is responsible for emotions of attachment, greed and envy. The chest is the seat of *kapha.*

A balance among the three elements, *tridosha,* is necessary for health. *Vāta* moves, whereas *kapha* and *pitta* are immobile. All the three govern the metabolical activities: anabolism (*kapha*), catabolism (*vāta*) and metabolism (*pitta*). If *vāta* is out of balance, catabolism will be disturbed. Excess *pitta* disturbs metabolism, excess *kapha* increases the rate of anabolism and excess *vāta* creates emaciation (catabolism). In childhood *kapha* elements are predominant, in adulthood *pitta* elements are most apparent, and in old age *vāta* is most prominent as the body begins to deteriorate.

On the mental planes, the three *doshas* correspond to the three *gunas*: *Sattva, Rājas* and *Tāmas. Sattva* expresses essence, understanding, purity, clarity, compassion and love. *Rājas* implies movement, aggressiveness and extroversion. *Tāmas* manifests in ignorance, inertia, heaviness and dullness. Individuals of *sattva* temperament have healthy bodies and are religious; of *rājas* temperament are interested in business, prosperity, power, prestige and position. They enjoy wealth and are generally extrovert; of *tāmas* temperament are lazy, selfish and capable of destroying others. They are unreligious, and their activities are egotistical. These three subtle mental energies are responsible for behavioural patterns and they may be altered or improved through the practice of spiritual disciplines such as yoga. Knowledge in Ayurvedic science combined with yoga can assist and guide the individual towards a more balanced mental and physical way of living.

Good health is created when all the *tridoshas* are in perfect equilibrium. When there is a disorder in the balance of *vāta-pitta-kapha* the seven *dhātus—Rasa* (plasma), *Rakta* (blood), *Rausha* (muscle tissue), *Meda* (adipose tissue), *Asthi* (bone tissue), *Majja* (bone marrow, nerve tissue) and *Shukra* (semen, reproductive tissue)—are directly affected. This equilibrium can be achieved by yoga and regulating dietary habits. If one has good health, one will have sound mind, which is essential for concentration and meditation.

According to Ayurveda the practice of yoga, which is a spiritual science of life, is a very important, natural, preventive measure to ensure good health. Ayurveda and Yoga are sister sciences. If Ayurveda is the science of the body, Yoga is a holistic science of the whole system. It is not merely directed to the spiritual aspects of human living. Yoga brings a natural state of tranquillity which is equilibrium. All the eight limbs of Yoga touch upon the ethical, physical, psychological and spiritual aspects of human life. The *Yama* and *Niyama* are essential for a clear, clean ethical living. The *āsana* and the *Prāṇāyāma* have both preventive and curative value. They help to bring natural order and balance to the neuro-chromones and the metabolism and improve the endocrine metabolism and thus provide fortification against stress. At the psychological level both *Pratyāhāra* and *Dhārana* help man achieve purity in mind, which is a must for *Dhyāna* at the spiritual level. Thus Yoga is a holistic science which aims at a complete transformation of human life, and recreates a new life based on harmony and tranquillity.

While practising Yoga, yogis may temporarily suffer from physical disorders because of releasing of disease producing toxins in the body. Employing Ayurvedic diagnosis and treatments, the yogis may effectively deal with these disorders. Similarly, Ayurveda indicates which type of yoga is suitable for each person according to his particular constitution. For example, a person of *Pitta* constitution should not perform the head stand posture for more than one minute. If he does, it results in mental disorientation. A person of *Vāta* constitution should not perform the shoulder stand for a long time as it exerts too much weight on the seventh cervical vertebra. A person of *Kapha* constitution should not perform the hidden lotus posture for an extended time because it causes direct pressure on the adrenal glands. Similarly, in *Prāṇāyāma* a person with *Pitta* constitution should perform left nostril breathing, a person with *Kapha* constitution right nostril breathing and a person with *Vāta* constitution alternate nostril breathing. A list of yoga postures for important *Vāta, Pitta* and *Kapha* ailments is provided here as follows:

Yogāsanas for Vāta

Constipation: Sarvāngāsana, Paschimottāsana, Tādāsana, Trikonāsana, Vrikshāsana, Ustrāsana, Uktāsana, Pādangustāsana, Sirsāsana. Savāsana, Nādisodha Prānāyāma for ten minutes.

Backache: Sarvāngāsana, Paschimottāsana, Urdhva Mukha Paschimottāsana, Ardha Matsyendrāsana, Ustrāsana, Salabhāsana, Dhanurāsana, Viparita Chakrāsana, Sirsāsana.

Depression: Halāsana, Yoga Mudra, Tādāsana, Padmāsana, Savāsana, Nādisodha Prānāyāma for ten minutes.

Rheumatoid Arthritis: Trikonāsana, Virabhadrāsana, Ardha Chandrāsana, Salambha Sarvāngāsana, Halāsana, Dhanurāsana, Virāsana, Ardha Matsyendrāsana, Chakrāsana, Savāsana.

Headache: Halāsana, Yoga Mudra, Sarvāngāsana, Paschimottāsana, Sirsāsana, Savāsana, Nādisodha Prānāyāma without retention for ten minutes.

Insomnia: Dhanurāsana, Paschimottāsana, Uttanāsana, Sarvāngāsana, Savāsana, Nādisodhana and Bhastrika and Suryabheda Prānāyāma for ten minutes without retention.

Menstrual Disorders: Halāsana, Dhanurāsana, Bhujangāsana, Yoga Mudra, Paschimottāsana, Matsyendrāsana, Virāsana, Baddha Konāsana, Ardha Matsyendrāsana, Savāsana, Nādisodhana

Prānāyāma with retention for ten minutes and Uddiyana.

Yogāsanas for Pitta

Peptic Ulcer: Trikonāsana and its variations, Virabhadrāsana, Pādangustāsana, Pāda Hastāsana, Uttānāsana, Salambha Sarvāngāsana, Paschimottāsana, Ardha Matsyendrāsana, Dhanurāsana, Bhujangāsana, Mayurāsana, Sirsāsana, Savāsana, Nādisodha Prānāyāma for ten minutes.

Hypertension: Halāsana, Ardha Baddha Padma, Paschimottāsana, Virāsana, Siddhāsana, Padmāsana, Savāsana, Nādisodha Prānāyāma for ten minutes without retention.

Liver Disorders: Dhanurāsana, Paschimottāsana, Baddha Konāsana, Ardha Matsyendrāsana, Parāsana, Bhujangāsana, Sarvāngāsana, Ālambha Sarvāngāsana, Salabhāsana, Urdhva Dhanurāsana, Vrischikāsana, Nādisodhana Prānāyāma for ten minutes.

Yogāsanas for Kapha

Bronchitis: All standing positions, Paschimottāsana, Sarvāngāsana, Bhujangāsana, Gomukhāsana, Ardha Matsyendrāsana, Virāsana, Sputa Virāsana, Yoga Nidra, Salabhāsana, Dhanurāsana, Ustrāsana, Vrikshāsana, Nādisodha and Suryabheda Prānāyāma for ten minutes.

Sinus congestion/headache: Matsyendra or Ardha Matsyendrāsana, Halāsana, Dhanurāsana,

Pādahastāsana, Bhastrika and Nādisodhana Prānāyāma for ten minutes without retention.

Diabetes: Sarvāngāsana, Paschimottāsana, Virāsana, Sputa Virāsana, Dhanurāsana, Salabhāsana, Uttānāsana, Ardha Matsyendra, Urdhva Dhanurāsana, Mayurāsana, Hamsāsana, Nādisodhana Prānāyāma with retention for ten minutes.

Gastro-intestine Disorders: Sarvāngāsana, Pādangustāsana, Pādahastāsana, Uttānāsana, Ardha Baddha Padma, Paschimottāsana, Halāsana, Chakrāsana, Sputa Virāsana, Yoga Mudrāsana, Dhanurāsana, Mayurāsana, Urdhva Dhanurāsana, Savāsana, Nādisodhana Prānāyāma for ten minutes.

Sore throat: Sarvāngāsana, Ustrāsana, Dhanurāsana, Ardha Matsyendra, Paschimottāsana, Urdhva Dhanurāsana, Simhāsana, Nādisodhana Prānāyāma, Ujjayi and Bhastrika for ten minutes.

Asthma: The āsanas listed under bronchitis should be followed.

The *āsanas* listed for various disorders of *vāta, pitta* and *kapha* have to be learnt from a teacher in an orderly fashion. One should not practise these *āsanas* by reading books and seeing pictures. This will cause immense damage to the vital organs of the body. For maintaining good and balanced health, one can perform a few selected standing, sitting and lying postures on a regular basis. Yoga helps maintain the balance between *vāta, pitta* and *kapha* and check if there are any disorders. Thus Yoga clubbed with ayurveda will ensure good health which is essential for taking up the higher yoga—the real spiritual life leading to the realization of the ultimate reality, that is, Brahman.

We now come to the last part of this article for our consideration, that is, food, which is an integral part of yoga-ayurvedic cycle. Ayurveda teaches that each individual has the power to heal himself and food plays a vital role here. Food has its direct effect on human thinking and emotional attitudes, and it creates *Tamasic, Rajasic* and *Sattvic* gunas. It has been unanimously approved that generally *sattvic* food which is purely vegetarian (which does not include even eggs) in character is recommended for attaining disease-free life and longevity and leading a spiritual life. Ayurveda recommends a balanced *sattvic* food which should contain all vitamins, minerals, carbohydrates, and fibres in equal proportion. Similarly, it does not recommend excess eating. It says that a human being should half-fill his/her stomach with properly cooked solid food free from spices, chillies and salt, free from strong, pungent and sour properties, and one-fourth with water and the remaining one-fourth should be left as enough empty space for the food to move freely without any discomfort.

Further, it recommends food that is helpful or harmful for each constitution. For instance, dry fruits, apples, melons, potatoes, tomatoes, egg plant, ice cream, beef, peas and green salad aggravate *vāta.* So, a person of *vāta* constitution should not take these foods in excess. Conversely, sweet fruits, avocados, coconuts, brown rice, red cabbage, bananas, grapes, cherries and oranges are beneficial for people of *vāta* constitution. Similarly, *pitta dosha* will be caused by spicy foods, peanut, butter, sour fruits, bananas, papayas, tomatoes and garlic. Foods that inhibit *pitta* are mangoes, oranges, pears, plums, sprouts, green salad, sunflower seeds, asparagus and mushrooms. Bananas, melons, coconuts, dates, papayas, pineapples and dairy products increase *kapha*. However, dry fruits, pomegranates, basamati rice, sprouts are beneficial for people of *kapha* constitution.

During summer when the temperature is high people tend to perspire excessively. *Pitta* predominates at that time. Hence it is not advisable to eat hot, spicy or pungent foods, because they will aggravate *pitta*. During autumn, when the wind is high and dry, more *vāta* will be present in the atmosphere. At this time, one should avoid dry fruits and high protein foods that increase *vāta*. Winter is the season of *kapha*. During this period one should avoid cold drinks, ice creams, cheese and yoghurt. Such foods will increase *kapha*.

Ayurveda also tells us that unless we feel hungry, do not eat, and unless we feel thirsty, do not drink. We should not eat when we feel thirsty, and drink when we feel hungry. When we are hungry, the digestive fire is enkindled. If we drink at this time, the liquid will dissolve the digestive enzymes and the *agni* will be reduced. Ayurveda also suggests that we do not drink water half-an-hour before taking food and avoid drinking water while eating. Proper munching of food will create juice in the mouth which will remove any sticking or blocking of food in the throat. Similarly, Ayurveda tells us that we should take water two hours after eating our food. This will necessitate proper digestion and good absorption of food in the body. The amount of food eaten at a meal should be the equivalent of two handfuls of food. If we eat more the stomach will expand and demand additional food. Overeating causes toxins in the digestive tract, it becomes poison.

It is food that nourishes the body, mind and consciousness. How we eat is very important. While eating we should sit cross-legged and straight with the spine erect and avoid watching television or reading or talking. We must focus our mind upon food and chew properly and relish the taste slowly. It is important that one eats at moderate speed. This is an experience. All this is meditation. It is not simply sitting cross-legged in a corner and watching our breath or thought-process. Meditation is a comprehensive term. It includes everything, every aspect of our life, every action and movement. Eating in this way will nourish our body, mind and consciousness and will also enhance longevity.

A few words about fasting. No fasting is required for a person whose constitution of *vāta-pitta-kapha* is well balanced. However, fasting has its own purpose. It eliminates unnecessary toxins in the body, thus purifies body, mind and soul. In fasting body becomes light, mind becomes soft, which will further strengthen the spiritual life. Once in a week a mild fasting may be undertaken which would make us realize the importance of food as well as the imperativeness of light body which is essential for spiritual *sādhana.*

Before a fast is undertaken, due consideration should be given to the individual constitution. A person of *vāta* constitution should not observe fasting for more than three days. A fast for more than four days will aggravate *pitta.* Persons with *kapha* constitution can observe prolonged fasts. They will feel a pleasant sensation of increased lightness, greater awareness and an opening of consciousness. Clarity and understanding will improve. During fasting, for persons with *vāta* and persons with *pitta* constitution pomegranate juice is recommended, and for persons with *kapha* constitution, apple juice is recommended.

What happens during fasting is that the digestive system comes to a rest. Which means the digestive fire (*agni*) becomes active and since there is no food to digest, it slowly burns away the long existing toxins in the intestines. Ayurveda also tells us that during fasting we can take decoction made of ginger, black pepper, a little jaggery and curry which have medicinal value which may naturalise toxins in the body. It will help enkindle *agni* which will burn away toxins. And fasting is a must during fever, cold, constipation or arthritic pain. For a normal healthy person, a warm water fast (one to two quarters per day) is advisable at least once in a week. This tones up the digestive system.

Ultimately Yoga and Ayurveda, if followed sincerely in our life, will prepare us for higher spiritual life. Whatever the ultimate goal of these two ancient sister sciences may be, it should be noted that a moderate, regulated, systematic, harmonious and rhythmical life is necessary for leading a happy life on this planet. For this, knowledge in Yoga and Ayurveda is a must and will help evolve a more meaningful and purposeful life in the world.

Unfortunately, in the fast changing world of life-styles, these two ancient sciences have been neglected in our country which is the bedrock of the world's greatest culture and civilization. Conversely, it is gaining momentum in the West. What is most disheartening and saddening to note is that the original standards and purity of these two ancient sciences have been highly diluted and neutralised by a few people with half knowledge to suit their selfish ends.

The real spirit of these ancient sciences which our great sages had preserved and lived in has been slowly eroded by ultra techniques which, unfortunately, to our utter shame, have been identified with the great tradition. The time has come for us to unearth the treasures of these two great ancient sciences and the true spirit hidden therein which Indian sages have given to humanity as legacies and preserve it and perpetuate it by living truly.

17

YOGA: A SCIENCE OF RELAXATION

Modern man is in constant stress and strain. He has more unsolved problems than solved and more unfulfilled desires than fulfilled. As a result he lives in despondency and despair. He does many unwanted things. He thinks unnecessarily over the petty, frivolous things that actually do not concern him. He broods over the past without deriving any benefit. He lives in expectation of what he does. He is more worried about his future, though not the present. He overreacts to various trivial human situations. In utter anxiety, he does things haphazardly and thereafter worries over things that have not happened to him. He is very much perturbed and disintegrated. The result of all this is that he is losing a lot of energy, vigour and strength. Man does not realize this simple truth. He has totally forgotten the great utility of conservation of energy. He has equally forgotten the principle of relaxation, that in a state of relaxation, energy is not wasted but properly channelled and conserved.

Modern man is not relaxed. He does not see the two active principles that every act proceeds from relaxation and that in relaxation energy is stored up and conserved. The vast majority of humanity do not have a comprehensive understanding of this beautiful science of relaxation simply because they have never looked at themselves—the manner in which they talk and do things. A look at himself will reveal what sort of man he is whether he is a split or an integrated whole being. Well, modern man is complex, debased and dehumanised, and not a man of integrity. He has lost harmony, the music in life. Nature, on the other hand, is harmonious, full of music. Man is discordant, out of tune with nature. In nature all things are perfectly relaxed, all animals and birds live in a state of harmony and relaxation. Therefore, they enjoy perfect peace and harmony. Look at dogs and cats in our home—how they sit quietly and relaxed. Man, I think, has to learn a great deal from these tiny creatures whom we never care to look at.

What is relaxation? During relaxation every part of body is almost at rest. During rest, all nervous system is relaxed, released from fatigue and lethargy. Every cell in the body is infused with fresh energy. It is conserved. No energy is wasted and dissipated. All muscles under stress and strain depreciate quickly; lose their vitality, vigour and strength. In sound sleep relaxation is total and complete. In disturbed sleep or dreamy sleep relaxation does not take place. It is partial and incomplete. The person feels tired, and exhausted on waking up.

When does relaxation take place? Exercise is necessary for health. Relaxation is equally necessary.

If relaxation is not maintained along with exercise, sound health cannot be maintained. Similarly, after strenuous work, muscles and nerves get tired. They need rest so as to recoup the energy. Or else energy gets wasted. The quality of relaxation also depends on the mental poise of the person. A man who is more worried and depressed cannot relax well. He is more disturbed and split. Relaxation can also take place at will. If the body and mind get tired, they need at once rest. It is better to rest a while and proceed. If on the other hand taxed heavily with work, it would be disastrous on the nervous system.

Relaxation is an art. One must know when one should get relaxed. This requires constant awareness of body and mind. It is a great discipline. It is an exact science. Yogis know this science well. They are perfect masters of this science. They never waste their energy. They know how to conserve energy. They do not experience fatigue. They do not act on impulses and instincts. They know pretty well that such impulsive actions cause high tension in nerves, muscles and brain. While a large number of people in the mundane world are slaves of impulses, and hence, they do not enjoy peace of mind.

Relaxation is of two kinds, viz., mental and physical. Physical relaxation pertains to muscles and nerves of the body, whereas mental relaxation to mind. Mind has its influence on body. In fact, the body is a mould prepared by the mind for its enjoyment. You are what your mind is. Mind has no existence apart from thoughts. Mind in Patanjali's *Yoga Sūtras* is identified with Pure Consciousness (*chit*), untainted by thoughts (*vrittīs*). As long as man is attached to these *vrittīs* or identifies himself with them, he is not freed, he cannot know the state of Pure Consciousness, the true nature of his self. Relaxation is impossible in such a state. The ultimate goal of yoga and that of all spiritual practices is *Chitta Vrittī nirodhah.* If a man achieves this state, he is totally and completely relaxed and freed. Yogis know this state by practice of meditation. A true yogi never identifies himself with *vrittīs.* Though he may act and experience, he is never touched by the fruits. There is no ego to experience. He is constantly aware of consciousness, completely, and he lives in it every moment. Thus, a yogi is totally and completely relaxed, balanced, peaceful and harmonious.

Any relaxation is inclusive of both physical and mental. There is nothing like partial relaxation which brings no true relief to the whole system. Relaxation must always be total, complete and full. It cannot happen by effort. It cannot be learnt from others, nor can it be taught by anyone. He who knows himself knows the art of relaxation. It is the genuine and honest enquiry into one's own nature—how one acts, what one does and so on that will undoubtedly provide one with abundant energy and strength, peace and happiness.

Modern man cannot understand this art because he is caught in the vortex of confusion. The confusion is created by himself. Unless he is freed from this confusion of which he is the cause, he can hardly enjoy happiness and peace. How to achieve this? Well, there is no definite way. However, in Yogic science, the art of relaxation has been dealt with at great length. The one way of relaxing the muscles, nerves, etc., is through *Savāsana* (corpse pose). *Mrityāsana* is another name for this pose. This can be practised in the morning, in the evening and at night before going to bed. Anyone can practise it in any place. The technique is simple. Spread a soft blanket. Wear loose garments. Avoid thick, trendy clothes. This will prevent the skin from receiving the fresh air. Cotton clothes are preferable. In winter, one can go for warm clothes. Or else, the skin and the muscles get contracted due to contact with the chillness. As a result one may not achieve relaxation. Now, lie flat on your back. Keep the hands on the ground by the sides. Stretch the legs quite straight. Let the feet drop outwards. Close the eyes and breathe slowly. Relax all the muscles, nerves, organs, etc. Start the relaxation process from the toes. Then proceed to the calf-muscles, muscles of the back, chest, arm, forearm and hands, neck, face, etc. See that the abdominal organs, heart, chest and brain are also relaxed. Do not sleep. You will enjoy perfect peace, ease, comfort and relaxation. *Savāsana* combines pose and meditation. It gives relief, comfort and ease. This can be done for ten to fifteen minutes. After this, you will be wonderfully refreshed and rejuvenated. You will be more efficient and effective in whatever you do. Relaxation is very important in one's life. The muscles that are put under severe strain demand relaxation and rest. It is *savāsana* that promptly and efficiently ensures complete relaxation and rest.

Makarāsana (the crocodile posture) may be recommended for women for partial relaxation. Lie down on your abdomen with the front of the body in contact with the ground. Stretch the two legs at full length partially separated. Let the sole of your feet face the sky or the roof in a room. Fold your arms and rest your head on them with the face turned to either of the sides. Gently close your eyes and begin to watch your breathing. Work on the principle of 'Let go' and offer no resistance against the pull of gravity. Release all tension in the muscles. Direct your attention to the lower parts of your body—the toes, the calves, thighs, etc., and gradually move upwards to the head. Remain in this state, placid and motionless. Breathing should be slow, normal and rhythmic. This posture for women will yield muscular relaxation free from psychosomatic disorders and better sleep. Avoid numbness creeping in upon any part of the body due to prolonged immobility. This posture may be done after a heavy work and before lunch and supper. If one wants to put this posture after supper, one should not take heavy food. This will disturb the sleep. If one doesn't get sleep at night one can do this posture one or two hours after taking food. This posture should not be done immediately after taking food.

For office-goers and businessmen whose job is sedentary, a different kind of posture is recommended. One can sit and relax, apart from doing *savāsana* at home. Sit relaxed in a sofa or a chair. Adjust your legs, feet, arms and hands to a comfortable position. Keep your two feet loose and dangled on either side. Remove chappals or shoes, including socks. Untighten the belt around the waist. See that there is no pressure on the belly. This will make the breathing difficult. Keep your arms on the resting points of the chair. Let your fingers and palms dangle. Rest your head on the back of the chair. You can slightly tilt your head on the right side. This is the position. Release every contracted muscle. Let go. Watch your breathing. Breathe slowly and quieten your mind without giving room for unnecessary anxiety. Remain passive and get completely absorbed in your breathing for fifteen to twenty minutes. This will yield complete relaxation, release from tension and subjective experience of quietude. What is to be remembered in this posture is that one should be able to retain the posture for a considerable length of time without experiencing numbness and pain.

Instead of choosing a chair or a sofa, one can sit relaxed reclining against the wall with two legs set apart and let loose, and two hands resting on the thighs or on either side. In this posture also, the fingers and palms must be let loose and head is tilted on the right side. Women can do this with ease and comfort.

Mind is the product of what one eats. One's own character also depends on the type of food one takes every day. There is a saying which goes like this: Tell me what you eat, I shall tell your character. *Sattvic* food is advisable. It consists of cereals, milk, pulses, vegetables, dry fruit and seasonal fruit. These are easily digestible and non-irritant. They promote purity of mind and inner strength. They are more conducive for higher thinking and pure intelligence. They keep body and mind in harmony and give you a cool temperament. They help you have a good relaxation and sound sleep free from disturbances and nightmarish experiences.

Mental poise and calmness can be achieved through meditation. Nothing can be gained by anxiety, fear, tension and worry. On the contrary, a great deal of energy will be wasted through these lower emotions and feelings. Man must cleanse himself of all these emotions, whether positive or negative. *Yama* and *Niyama*, the first two limbs of *Astānga Yoga* will be of immense benefit in cleansing process. This cleansing process is an essential prerequisite for meditation. One can sit for twenty to thirty minutes daily both in the morning and evening and watch his thoughts, without disturbing or altering them. Let them come and go. You should merely watch them in a detached sense. Slowly and steadily, all thoughts recede and a vacuum is created. Remain in that state without experiencing anything in it, or expecting or anticipating something to happen. This should not be done with effort or at will or with over-anxiety. This kind of state for a few minutes, if practised sincerely and honestly, will give one immense mental peace, mental vigour and strength.

To conclude, relaxation is essential for every man who has become complex by virtue of his own creations. It is both an art and science. Relaxation achieves unruffled peace, abiding joy, bubbling vitality, vigour and strength in one's life. Yoga helps in realizing peace, harmony and happiness. Yoga is a science of relaxation; it is a perfect science in achieving the greatest and the maximum happiness, peace and freedom not only for one but for the whole humanity on the earth.

18

FOOD AND YOGIC SĀDHANA

The first virtue of *Niyama* is *saucha* or purity. According to the yogic philosophy the whole of the universe, seen or unseen, is a manifestation of the Divine Consciousness. Hence, to the enlightened sage or saint everything is pure and sacred. From this higher point of view nothing can therefore be considered impure in the absolute sense. But in relation to our ordinary life, pure and impure are relative and functional, and not absolute. A man is pure if it enables and helps him serve efficiently as an instrument of the expression of Divine Consciousness. If he is impure, it impedes the full expression of Divine Life. Purification, therefore, in yogic philosophy means the maintenance and transformation of man in such a manner that he can serve as a vehicle to bring in Divine Consciousness.

Purity, though functional and relational, depends on three factors: the nature of man, the structural body-mind complex and the sensitiveness. All the three are important. If we want to bring down divine consciousness into human consciousness, we must provide the right kind of body-mind complex material. But, as such, body-mind complex material is coarse, it has to be refined, made subtle. This can be brought about by supplying the right kind of food.

Next to air and water the most important requisite for a human being is food. The object of food is not to merely fill the belly and fulfil the tastes of the tongue, but to develop the mind and character too. Food is closely related to thinking, character and deeds. The kind of food one eats determines one's character.

According to the yogic system food is divided into three classes—*Tamasic, Rajasic* and *Sattvic* and only those which are considered *sattvic* are allowed in yogic *sādhana.* Meat, alcohol and so many other accessories of a modern diet make the physical body utterly useless for the yogic life. These kinds of food coarsen the body and mind which is not fit for receiving divine consciousness.

What is *sattvic* food? It is purely vegetarian which includes fresh fruits, nuts, dried fruits, vegetables, pulses and milk. It should be balanced, nutritional and energising. It should improve our body's defence system or immunity from disease and not interfere in expulsion of waste materials and toxins. It should not contain substances which are disease inducing, which destroy health and which create excitement and affect us emotionally, psychologically and create imbalance and lack of self-control and discipline in the body. The normal intake of food should contain between 2100 and 2700 calories and the vegetarian food contains all types of nutritional ingredients in sufficient quantity. Flesh foods induce incurable diseases and shorten the life span.

How much one should eat? Overeating and starvation are two extremes. Eating moderately and only when we feel hungry is a healthy sign and recommended in yogic life. We must remember that "we eat to live and not live to eat", those who eat more than their appetite become victims of indigestion, constipation, obesity and other ailments. Overeating is the main cause of most diseases. Yogic system says that only half of one's stomach should be filled with food, one quarter with water, and the remaining quarter should be left empty so as to facilitate the food to move freely. If one follows this principle, one feels more comfortable to do spiritual *sādhana*. Also the *sādhaka* should eat sparingly and not whenever his tongue titillates. Shastras say that one who eats three times is a *rogi*, two times a *bhogi* and one time a *yogi*; and a *maha yogi* is one who eats rarely.

Our body is a wonderful complex machine which is constantly engaged in many activities like breathing, digesting, circulating, purifying, expelling, etc. This mechanism works efficiently only if we eat less and moderately. More food creates pressure on the machine. So, it will wither away quickly. The less we eat the more efficiently the machine will work and last longer time. "Food is made for us and we are not made for food." Hence to remain healthy our principle should be "eat less, have more health".

Good health is not given nor to be procured, but to be attained; and it is an essential condition for yogic life.

In nature herbivorous animals eat only grass and leaves; carnivorous animals only flesh. The lion will never eat grass even if it is hungry and a cow will never take flesh even if it is starving. Similarly, they do not eat round the clock. Only when the tiger is hungry it goes for hunting. But man contravenes nature. No human being can live only on flesh because that is not his complete food and also it reduces the life span. Even Eskimos who are compelled to subsist on meat have an average life span of only thirty years. But man can live a long and healthy life on purely vegetarian diet.

Scientists have time and again proved that man is not a carnivorous animal but a descendant of fruit eating animal. Primitive man though lived on flesh has gradually evolved. He is not the same what he was millions of years ago. Every sage and saint has given long sermons on the baneful effects of flesh eating. A flesh eater is not fit for spiritual life. Jesus Christ says, "whosoever eats flesh of an animal is actually eating his own flesh himself." George Bernard Shaw, a distinguished English dramatist of the twentieth century, once remarked: "Meat eaters are like walking graves of slaughtered animals." Chanakya observed, "those who eat meat or drink alcohol are animals in human form and a burden on earth."

So, what is required for yogic *sādhana* is *sattvic* food which gets rid of the undesirable material in the body and makes it sufficiently refined. The purification of the subtler vehicles which serve as instruments for the expression of divine consciousness is brought by food. *Sattvic* food eliminates undesirable thoughts and emotions which cause disturbances. It replaces those negative thoughts, emotions and feelings by thoughts and emotions of higher and subtler nature. A pure mind can think pure thoughts and feel pure emotions. Therefore, it becomes difficult for it to entertain undesirable thoughts and emotions in the same way as it is difficult for an impure mind to entertain high and noble thoughts and emotions.

Purification is a positive practice. The more one purifies oneself the more one becomes subtler. Subtleness is very important in spiritual life. It leads to greater sensitiveness. Each cell in human body becomes highly responsive which happens only on purification of undesirable toxic elements. Divine consciousness is pure, and hence it can manifest in human consciousness when it is purified. Here, food plays a vital role. Seventy to eighty per cent of our impurities arise from the intaking of food. Hence, it is given more importance in yogic *sādhana.* Right kind of vegetarian food, nutritious, balanced and energising, can alone create a congenial spiritual atmosphere in human body and mind.

19

YOGA AS AN ART OF SOCIAL RECONSTRUCTION

To many Hindus, Yoga is known as an integral part of Hindu tradition. To non-Hindus too Yoga is identified with Hindu religion. Both conceptions seem to have taken strong roots in the minds of Hindus and non-Hindus. It is, in fact, part of *Sanātana Dharma.* Patanjali did not divide it 2000 years ago. He described Yoga as *sārvabhauma.* '*Bhauma*' means the world, '*sarva*' means all. Yoga is a universal culture. Just as it works on the whole of the individual, so it is meant for the development of the whole of mankind on the physical, mental, intellectual and spiritual levels. Further, Yoga is known by almost everyone as a philosophy or religion. This idea also is wrong, though it matters much for academicians. Patanjali never conceived it as a religion. For him it is a way of life. It aims at the development of integral personality which in turn prepares man for greater spiritual life which is above all religions. In this sense, Yoga is above all religions, it is a religion of all religions, it is a science of all sciences.

Very few know that Yoga is also an art. Indeed, it is an art of all arts. It embraces all arts and is thus the fundamental art. But this art has nothing to do with the acquisition of skill as is the case in all other art forms. All art forms are mental creations. One can acquire greater dexterity in any art form by perseverance and practice. Yoga is not an art in this sense. It has nothing to do with skill, though it is part of Yoga. It is an art that goes beyond mind and touches the 'inner'. It is an art of the 'inner'. It is, hence, a spiritual art. It is a total art because it embraces every part of human body. Whereas in other art forms, mind and its trickery creations play a predominant role. In Yoga art, every part of human body is taken into account and an integration is achieved. It aims at the total integration, unification and harmony of human body, mind and the inner being.

The art of Yoga deals with living. Living is an art. The art of living is a great art—greater than all other arts because each performing art or fine art deals with one aspect of human creation. Hence, they are segmentary. Whereas the art of living is total, comprehensive and inclusive of everything else. It is not momentary, but moving from one moment to another with complete and total awareness. Hence, Yoga is the fundamental art. It deals with the art of living in its totality and not fragments. Hence, a Yogi is a greater artist than all other artists. His living itself is more creative, though he doesn't create like other artists. He makes his life more creative, dynamic, thrilling and exciting. He enjoys, unlike the other artists, every moment of life.

While other art forms are directed to the objective world, Yoga is purely concerned with the subjective world. There is no objective world without the subject. Everything is subjective. Yoga proceeds from the subject—the self. It helps man understand his own complex self. Understanding one's own self is not an easy task. It requires tremendous will power, courage and constant awareness. It does not involve segmentary understanding. It is total comprehension of the self—its mechanism, its intricacies, its nuances. A Yogi constantly makes an effort, and his effort is *sādhana* and this *sādhana* is a whole lifetime process. Sri Aurobindo thus calls "all life is Yoga". It includes all life on the earth. Therefore, all Yoga is art. Whereas other artists act in inspiration, transport themselves into a world of their own and create. But, soon, as the process of creation is over, they plummet into their own petty self. Therefore, an artist is an artist so long as he creates, while a Yogi is an artist for the whole of his life.

Yoga deals with man-making. It is the building of a whole man. Yoga is not mere postures and breathing. Nor is it a mere handbook of instructions as to how to live in a jungle, in a world negating retirement. It is not an impractical idealism—nor a dreamy ideology. But it deals with achieving equanimity, composure and ease at all times, and thus most effectively come to meet always his own personal, social and national problems. It tells us how man can live a better life in the world, and how he can gain a mastery over his destiny. Yoga is a great science, and it has a glorious utility in the world. It is not concerned with rituals and ceremonies, but it helps one discover in oneself a new strength and vitality to face one's own challenges in life, and provides a new world of inward courage of conviction to live honestly serving others. It deals with the wholeness of man. It shapes and moulds the whole being. It transforms man from his crude, despicable, diabolical form into a fine human being who can live with greater integrity, honesty, simplicity and truthfulness in the world. Such a man can easily influence his fellow beings and affect the society in a positive way. He can govern himself in the best possible way and he who governs himself needs no governance from outside. Good governance comes from within and that will remain steadfast and everlasting. That which comes from within has tremendous moral force and conviction and hence, it can never be erased so easily by outward forces. A Yogi needs no governance of whatsoever from outside, he leads a happy life. He who relies on governance from outside for his moral conduct will always suffer in conflicts. Yoga offers good governance of oneself.

Yoga is also distinguished from the other arts in another dimension. Generally, art is an expression of the inner—the inner being, the emotional upheavals that happen to us in our day-to-day life. An artist uses these emotions and transforms them into artistic expression. Whereas a Yogi works to conquer them and cultivates empathy, compassion, friendliness, joy and indifference towards happiness and sorrow and service in order to achieve complete harmony with the cosmos. Yoga is a perfect art of the rhythmical movement of the inner. Though it

doesn't express itself in any artistic form its dynamism is visible, and felt in every moment of living. Finally, he tries to realize *satyam, sivam* and *sundaram* and lives in it. Thus, he divinises his life. Whereas an art, though gives us aesthetic pleasure which is beyond sensual pleasure, still suffers from the lack of sublime which is divine. Yoga doesn't suffer from the lower. It aims at the higher life. The purpose of Yoga is to divinise life.

Such a man-making art is essential for social reconstruction. Any social reconstruction or reformation should start from the individual, who is a basic unit of society. Or any social reconstruction with structural changes in human institutions becomes incomplete unless and until it is accompanied by individual reconstruction. Yoga offers this reconstruction at the individual level. Yoga is firstly for individual growth, but through individual growth, society and community develop. It offers a solution to all problems of humanity. It rings a total change in life so that as individuals with a greater stability of mind we may achieve a greater harmony in our personal life, thereby in social life too. Individual growth is a must, if society needs growth in real life sense and Yoga develops each individual, if followed by letter and spirit.

Yoga is an integral art. It can be dealt from ethical, physical, psychological and spiritual levels. From the point of view of physical, Yoga removes toxins from the system and improves its health. From the psychological point of view, it quietens the mind. From the spiritual point of view, it takes the

individual beyond mind and merges with the Cosmic. All the eight limbs of Yoga are made into ethical, physical, psychological and spiritual. These are gradual steps leading one to the other, finally to a greater spiritual height. Ethical Yoga comprises *Yama* and *Niyama.* These two are like the roots and the trunk of the tree. *Yama* principles include *ahimsā* (non-violence), *satya* (truthfulness), *āsteya* (freedom from avarice), *brahmacharya* (control of sensual pleasures) and *aparigrāha* (non-covetousness) and *Niyama* principles comprise *saucha* (cleanliness), *santosa* (contentment), *tapas* (austerity), *svādhyāya* (self-study) and *Īshvara-Pranidhāna* (surrender through devotion). The physical Yoga comprises *āsanas* and *Prānāyāma. Āsana* is the art of positioning the body which has two aspects, posing and reposing. Both have to be balanced to achieve good results in the body. Ultimately, *āsanas* create a healthy body which is essential for mind to concentrate and meditate. The leaves are the *Prānāyāma.* As the leaves create the tree and provide nourishment for its healthy growth, so *Prānāyāma* feeds and aerates the cells, nerves, organs, intelligence and consciousness of the human system. Psychological Yoga includes *Pratyāhāra* and *Dhārana.* The bark is *pratyāhāra* translated as withdrawal of senses. The sap of the tree is *Dhārana,* that is, concentration or complete attention which flows within the branches and the trunk of the tree towards the root. The spiritual Yoga comprises *Dhyāna* and *Samādhi.* The flower of the tree is *Dhyāna,* meditation, which balances the body, mind and intellect. And the last of the tree is fruit, which is *Samādhi,* wherein the ego is completely

derived from the Sanskrit word '*yuj*' meaning 'to join', 'to yoke', 'to combine' or 'to bring together'. Hence, it conveys the sense of union. According to Hindu philosophy of which the science of yoga is an integral part, the human soul or the *jīvātman* is a partial expression of the Over-soul or *Paramātman*, the manifested universe. Although in essence the two are the same and indivisible, the *jīvātma* has become subjectively separated from the *paramātman* and is destined, after going through an evolutionary cycle in the manifested universe, to become united with Him again in Consciousness, as well as the mental process and discipline through which this union is attained are both called Yoga.

Before man can establish communion, harmony, order and peace with Nature, he must at the lower level achieve complete integration within himself. Without this man cannot attain harmony with Nature. If he is wholly integrated both in body and mind, he is one with Nature or Cosmos. For this, psychological transformation is necessary.

Yoga helps man understand himself without any prejudice, look inwardly without any malice. Yoga is knowing oneself. Self-knowledge implies psychological transformation. It is the constant awareness of the workings of mind. This is meditation. Meditation does not imply that one should watch one's own mind by adopting a posture for some time. It is a continuous watching or observation of one's own mind—how one talks, walks, reads, writes and so on. By watching continuously, one can eliminate or thwart the *Vrittīs*. When these *Vrittīs* are eliminated man attains pure consciousness which is his true nature.

Self-knowledge alone can bring tranquillity and happiness. One should be extremely vigilant in doing things. This results in integration of personality. Once man achieves this in his life, he sees unity in Nature. He becomes one with Nature. This is true Yoga.

Self-awareness

Self-knowledge is the negation of all knowledge. It is the end of all knowledge and the beginning of wisdom. It is an undivided mind. It is an insight into oneself. It is the knowing of every moment of thought. It is right education. In this right education, man becomes the teacher as he watches, and the taught as he himself analyses and understands, and emerges out of it as a new human being. Self-knowledge is complete awareness.

In this awareness, there is learning and understanding which become endless. All anxieties, painful memories, deep urges, anger, fear, frustration, despair, jealousy, pride are rooted out. This awareness does not interfere with or suppress or pass any judgement on what happens and what is revealed before its watchful eyes. The principle of ego, 'I', is totally obliterated. From this comes new freedom and happiness which are eternally present in Nature. One becomes merged in the totality of freedom that is pure state and unsullied.

The individual ego has many dimensions. It is like a mirage, a false individuality. When this is totally annihilated, man will be free from the bondage of cause and effect. What results is a state of mind in which there is no conflict. It is a pure state. Whatever is done in this state is unfragmented.

Conclusion

Yoga, if practised sincerely, works tremendously on each individual at the physical and mental levels. It can make people divine. It brings peace for man and all humanity. Through individual peace, community develops, society flourishes. Happiness can be established in the world. Yoga is a science, a philosophy and an art. It is not a creed or a dogma as it is sometimes misunderstood. It is a way of living. It cuts through all divisions and differences. Once an aspirant is firmly established in yoga, peace and happiness become his property. He then becomes a true property. He then becomes a true yogi—a true human being.

INDEX